A gift for:

_____

From:

_____

Date:

_____

A Christmas Wonderland:
Stories, Verse, and Thoughts to Cheer Your Heart

ISBN 0-8307-4202-6
Copyright © 2006 Mark Gilroy Communications, Inc.
All rights reserved.
Printed in China

Design by Greg Jackson, Thinkpen Design LLC, Springdale, AR

A Christmas Wonderland

Stories, Verse, & Thoughts to Cheer Your Heart

Regal

From Gospel Light
Ventura, California, U.S.A.

Contents

Christmas waves a magic wand
over this world, and behold, everything
is softer and more beautiful.

NORMAN VINCENT PEALE

Holiday Cheer

He told them to celebrate these days
with feasting and gladness and by
giving gifts to each other and to the poor.

ESTHER 9:22 NLT

Throughout the world, Christmas is a magical time. Just the sight of neighborhood lights makes us suddenly feel like children, and there's nothing better than getting together with family and friends for holiday treats and favorite songs and carols. However we celebrate, there's something about Christmas that cheers our hearts like no other time of year.

A good holiday is one spent
among people whose notions of time
are vaguer than yours.

J.B. PRIESTLEY

Angel with an Accent

BEVERLY BUSH SMITH

Five days till Christmas, and the last thing I needed was a stranger in the house.

I'd abandoned my kitchen in chaos from a much-interrupted baking binge in order to dress for a neighbor's holiday party. Now, with one foot in my pantyhose, I answered the phone to hear a heavily-accented male French voice asking for our son, Bryan, who'd lived in France for a year.

Bryan was out of town, not to be reached for two days, and I was beginning to think he'd invited everyone he met abroad to come visit us in Southern California.

There followed an exchange of fractured English (the Frenchman's) and fractured French (mine). Yes, he would like to stay with us. I hung up, doubting my sanity. I'd now have another body in the house for Christmas, in addition to our two sons, their girlfriends, and my husband's parents.

But the day after the movie-star handsome, dark-haired Jacques arrived, I began to learn he was not simply another body, but a willing, able, and generous addition to the household. That afternoon, he asked, "You want that I prepare the crêpes for dinner?" Did I ever.

He indicated he would make them both for the entrée and for dessert. I'd need only to fix a salad. Then he wrote this explanation for me: "Mattefin. It's the name of crêpes of Alps."

He had a lovely touch with the delicate glorified pancakes, though the first two landed in the dish of George, our cat, as Jacques fine-tuned the heat of the stove. His special "invention" once each crêpe was turned was to break a single egg on top, stir it with a wooden spoon, then sprinkle a handful of Emmental cheese on top. He rolled the crêpe just before the egg was completely set, producing a delectably moist creation, no sauce needed.

Jacques finished the dessert crêpes with both orange-enhanced jam and chocolate sauce. Luscious.

The following day our visitor's next culinary offer produced "a dish of my region, Grenoble," a peasant dish, *pommes de terre gratin dauphinois*. Jacques thinly sliced potatoes to bake with milk, butter, bits of bacon, and plenty of Gruyère cheese.

Oven temperature was his only challenge. "They are still swimming," he reported, moving his hands in a pantomimed breast stroke before turning the heat higher. The hearty, savory potatoes were well worth the wait.

Jacques' talents extended beyond the kitchen. When I plugged in a string of Christmas tree lights and they failed to twinkle, Jacques assessed the situation with an "I fix." And it was done. When I struggled to create the centerpiece of Rome apples that looked so easy in the magazine, Jacques watched and suggested, "Maybe like this?" And he was right.

The day before Christmas, Jacques caught me as I began to assemble the ingredients for a baked Alaska. Did I "want that" he fix a *mousse au chocolat* for Christmas dinner? I noted that I'd already started the dessert.

"Eh bien, then we have two desserts."

Obviously, we didn't need two, and just as obviously, he was determined. I surrendered. And relaxed.

Christmas morning, as I cooked our traditional breakfast sausage and sliced my *stollen* coffee cake, Jacques appeared. "You want that I fix the eggs?"

"Fine," my husband answered. "Scrambled?"

Jacques scratched his head, frowning. "*Omelette?*"

I started to explain scrambled eggs and then decided, "Yes,

omelet. Wonderful."

Later, Jacques used a dozen egg whites to make his glorious, deeply chocolate mousse, then pondered the remaining yolks. "You want that I make the mayonnaise?"

Homemade mayonnaise. What a luxurious dip for the veggies before dinner.

At dinnertime, unsure if my standing rib roast had cooked enough, I consulted the chef, who made a microscopic cut with the tip of a boning knife.

"Off," he decreed over the oven knob.

"Not too rare?" I worried.

"Perfect," he pronounced.

And it was. So was the mayonnaise. And the mousse.

Marveling at how Jacques' presence enriched our Christmas celebration, I hoped he'd stay—and stay.

But the morning after Christmas, his backpack stood by the front door.

"I have brushed my teeth," he explained in French, "so I can smile my best to hitchhike to Tijuana, Mexico."

And so, with an embrace and a kiss on each cheek, he was gone. As I closed the door, a scripture from Hebrews flashed into my mind: "Do not forget to entertain strangers, for by so doing some people have entertained angels without knowing it" (Hebrews 13:2).

I stood in the kitchen, blinking. By welcoming this stranger, had we entertained an angel, one with a French accent who blessed us abundantly with his generous giving of himself? Perhaps I would never know—but my taste buds certainly thought so. ✶

Do not forget to entertain strangers,
for by so doing some people have entertained
angels without knowing it.

HEBREWS 13:2

At Christmas play and make
good cheer, for Christmas
comes but once a year.

THOMAS TUSSER

At Christmas Time

ENGLISH, TRADITIONAL

At Christmas time we deck the hall
With holly branches brave and tall,
With sturdy pine and hemlock bright
And in the Yule log's dancing light
We tell old tales of field and fight
    At Christmas time.

At Christmas time we pile the board
With flesh and fruit and vintage stored,
And mid the laughter and the glow
We tread a measure soft and slow,
And kiss beneath the mistletoe
    At Christmas time.

The most vivid memories
of Christmases past are usually
not of gifts given or received,
but the spirit of love, the special
warmth of Christmas worship,
the cherished little habits of the home.

LOIS RAND

Daddy's Christmas Trees

ANNE CULBREATH WATKINS

My father is the gruff, outdoorsy type. He'd rather hike through the woods than sit sedately inside a stuffy house any day. Never mind that he's nearly eighty years old, Daddy has a mind of his own and is quick to set straight anyone who suggests he slow down because of his age. He's on the stubborn side, set in his ways, and not a man prone to lavish displays of sentimentality. Despite his brusque demeanor, though, he absolutely adores getting together with us kids to celebrate holidays and birthdays.

After one holiday meal at my brother's house, inspired by Daddy's reminiscent ruminating, we decided to go for a walk down to the old place where we grew up, which lay just yards away. We had a hard time keeping up with all the memories my dad produced about the old house as we walked toward the lot. While the rickety frame house was long gone, there were still plenty of things to look at and remember in the yards that had surrounded it.

We were strolling leisurely around the property when Daddy pointed toward a scraggly row of cedar trees, each one bigger than the last. "Do you know what those are?" he asked me, grinning.

A rush of memories flooded my mind and I suddenly found myself transported back through the years to the Christmases we spent at this old place.

The very first Christmas tree I remember stood in the corner of our front room. The crisp scent of fresh cedar wafted throughout the house, and the sticky, prickly foliage was laden with glowing lights, ornaments, and tinsel. The tree stood carefully propped in a bucket of water to keep it alive, and I enjoyed swirling my fingers in the cool depths, inhaling the tree's wonderful aroma.

The day after Christmas, Daddy took the tree outside and planted it in the front yard where it joined a row of other cedars, Christmas trees from years gone by, that grew into a sturdy wall. I used to play behind that wall of trees, their thick, low-set branches shielding me from passing cars and providing a fragrant, albeit prickly, shelter.

Then, when I was six, we moved to Alabama, leaving behind the row of Christmas trees, and I wondered if Christmas in Alabama would be as wonderful as the ones I remembered in Ohio.

I soon discovered that Christmas in Alabama was different—for one thing, there was no snow. My child's mind worried that Santa would never find us or that the little Nativity scene we always set up would look out of place. Then Daddy stepped in.

A few days before Christmas, he went into the woods and returned with a small, shapely cedar which he set in a bucket of water in the living room. We decorated it with the same ornaments from past Christmases, along with colorful paper chains and stars we cut out of construction paper. The wise men smiled from the Nativity scene and it seemed to me as if they were thrilled to be celebrating the Christ Child's birthday in Alabama.

After the holidays, Daddy took the tree outside and, carefully lifting the root ball from the bucket, planted it in the yard beside the house, where it grew into a beautiful, full-bodied cedar. Each year, one more tree found its place in the row until there was a neat line of cedars, graduating in size from very small to very tall, standing point over the house.

Now, all these decades later, some of those same trees still stand on the grounds of the old home place, a matching one standing at Dad's place in Alabama. Who would have thought that my father, the gruff woodsman, would be sentimental enough to recycle our old Christmas trees into rows of living memories? Yet there they stand, two rows of memory-trees, testifying to the warm heart nestled inside the curt old man and reminding me of the magic of Christmas. ✴

For the happy heart, life is a continual feast.

PROVERBS 15:15 NLT

Here We Go A-Caroling

LETTIE KIRKPATRICK BURESS

The music of Christmas sets it apart from all other holidays. Beloved, ageless hymns speak of a holy birthday and faith, while cheerful tunes tell of the sights, sounds, and smells of Christmas. But what about the stories behind the songs? Here are condensed versions of the origins of five holiday favorites.

- "Silent Night" was written when the organ malfunctioned on Christmas Eve in 1818. Joseph Mohr, the assistant priest at St. Nicholas Church in Oberndorf, Austria, wrote the words, then persuaded his organist to set them to music for guitar and voice.

- "O Little Town of Bethlehem" was birthed in 1865 when Phillip Brooks was touring the Holy Land on Christmas Eve. He gazed at the shepherd's fields, looked at the town, and attended a local worship service. Three years later, he merged his memories of those events into the enduring song.

- "I Heard the Bells on Christmas Day" was born of the despair of Henry Wadsworth Longfellow. As the Civil War threatened to tear the United States apart, he grieved that evil seemed to be overcoming good and that strife had devoured peace. Then he heard the church bells ringing and penned this song declaring God's faithfulness.

- "We Three Kings" was written by John Henry Hopkins in 1857. Although the Bible actually reveals little about the men who traveled from the East to visit Jesus, Hopkins blended the Scriptures, church tradition, and legend. He immortalized in song these visitors from the East referred to in the Bible as "magi."

- "Angels from the Realms of Glory" was written by Scottish-born James Montgomery in the 1800s. Montgomery was dismissed from seminary because of his love for poetry. He became a newspaper editor in London and was twice imprisoned for writing controversial opinions. "Angels from the Realms of Glory" was written for his newspaper column. ✶

Speak to one another with psalms, hymns and spiritual songs.
Sing and make music in your heart to the Lord.

Ephesians 5:19

Christmas, children, is not a date.
It is a state of mind.

MARY ELLEN CHASE

A Country Christmas

ELAINE YOUNG MCGUIRE

I grew up in a small town perched atop the Cumberland Plateau in Tennessee, a blanket of rich green pastures and tall sugar maples. We lived in one of the new houses, a very modern orange brick home that Sunday drivers from the surrounding countryside drove by to ogle. My mother decorated the house beautifully each Christmas, and we often won the town's door decorating contest.

But as much as I loved December in my little town, I couldn't wait to spend Christmas with Daddy's family at the "home place" in Brush Creek.

According to custom, after Santa came on Christmas morning, we headed out to celebrate the holiday with Mother's family, all living near Nashville, before driving to rural Brush Creek later in the day. We would fellowship for a few hours at my aunt and uncle's gorgeous home overlooking their private lake, enjoying a formal country ham breakfast, my aunt's beautiful, magazine-worthy decorations, and more hugs than we could handle. And then we would embark on the hour-long drive to Grandmother's house.

The changing landscape fascinated me. Rocky terrain soon replaced the rolling green hills as large evergreens replaced the hardwoods. As the bridges across the Stones and Cumberland Rivers came into view, flanked by forests of cedar trees, it seemed perfectly natural to me, as the oldest child, to lead my twin sisters and brother in a loud, cheerful rendition of "Over the River and Through the Woods." The miles quickly melted away, just as quickly as the occasional Christmas snowfall.

Suddenly we saw the sign that read, "Welcome to Brush Creek," and after bouncing over the railroad tracks and turning to go down the steep hill toward Grandmother's white clapboard house, it was like we had time-traveled back a hundred years.

Our car bumped over the front sidewalk before pulling into park in the yard. Then my siblings and I catapulted out of the car and up the steps to the large porch, into the waiting arms of relatives, "There's Gilbert, Sara, and the kids! Merry Christmas! Come inside where it's warm." We knew that behind the slapping screen door waited huge helpings of acceptance and love, along with loads of good food and lots of fun.

My grandparents raised ten children in that old house, as well as a grandchild whose mother died young. There had always been room for one more, and the older children were taught and expected to help their younger siblings. Granddaddy owned a drugstore and general store, located just across the street from the house. I never knew him, yet I could always sense his presence when I visited the old house.

The Young family's entire world existed within just a few blocks: the house, grocery, church, train depot, and the two-room school where two of my aunts taught. The country doctor lived next door. Even the cemetery was just over the hill.

Grandmother's front door opened to a big dogtrot hallway, with two rooms on one side and three on the other. A stairway led to a tiny attic bedroom. In the back were a narrow, enclosed sun porch and a small bathroom. It was just that: a private room in which to bathe from a bowl. The house seemed to shrink when our whole extended family descended on it each Christmas Day.

Upon arrival, we assembled in the largest front room, pulling chairs in a circle near the coal-burning fireplace to chase away the chill. The fragrance of the large, hand-cut cedar tree, decorated with bubble lights, icicles, paper chains, and cranberry and popcorn chains, filled the air. Our gatherings were never about gifts, but all of us could expect one from Aunt Norma, my unmarried aunt who lived there with Grandmother. We knew it would be something inexpensive, useful, and sweet, like a comb or handkerchief, wrapped in the Sunday comics and tied up with curly red ribbon.

After gifts were unwrapped, it was time to eat our late dinner. Aunt Norma must have cooked for days to prepare enough food for us all, aided by all the aunts when they arrived. Each main dish and side was completely homemade, assembled from simple ingredients and several generous pinches of skill, time, and loving attention to detail.

We crowded into the dining room for the blessing, the children silently praying, *God, please let it be a short one!* Once the food was blessed, we quickly filled our old, sometimes cracked china plates and took them to empty spots throughout the house. We kids usually congregated on the stairs, even though the hall was not heated and we had to stay bundled up. We were never warned not to spill, and we were allowed to go back for seconds, including several desserts, without asking. After all, it was a holiday.

After the meal, the men retired to the living room fire, while the women and older girls headed to the kitchen. Some went to the side porch to draw water from the rain barrel, others set water pots to boiling, and a team of others washed and dried dishes and put them away, all the while laughing and sharing our lives together. Not only did we not envy the men, we didn't want them around to get in the way of the woman-talk.

Before too long, we wandered back to the crackling fire and sat again, sharing stories and jokes. Two preacher uncles and their wives told the best ones, but the kids were encouraged to participate too.

When boredom set in, the children returned to the stairs to play games. Our favorite was simple: One cousin hid a buckeye in one hand, both hands placed behind his back. When he turned his clenched fists before us, we each took a turn guessing which hand held the nut. We moved up or down the stairs, according to our lucky or unlucky guesses. The first to make it to the top and back down again was the proud winner of...nothing. Nonetheless, this game occupied us for hours.

When we grew older, we separated by age groups. I was thrilled the year my favorite cousin, Joann, deemed me the youngest older cousin. While the little ones continued games, we whispered secrets and later went for joyrides in Joann's truck, bouncing off the seat as we drove far too fast down into dips and up again along the country roads.

Grandmother died before I grew up, and so did Joann's daddy. Her mom sold their farm, and they bought the home place from Aunt Norma, who then moved to my hometown.

I never spent Christmas in Brush Creek after that, but when I visited Joann during the summer, I appreciated the new indoor bathroom, running water in the kitchen, and the gas space heaters. But we still loved washing our hair in rainwater from the big barrel out back and sharing talks late at night.

Over fifty years have passed, our own children are grown, and today Joann and I live in suburban Atlanta, twenty miles apart. We intend to spend more time together than we do, but when we do talk or visit, time stands still. We are two young girls again, chattering and sharing reminiscent stories of our Christmases at Brush Creek. ✳

> *Love each other with genuine affection,*
> *and take delight in honoring each other.*
>
> ROMANS 12:10 NLT

Heap on more wood! The wind is chill;

But let it whistle as it will,

We'll keep our Christmas merry still.

SIR WALTER SCOTT

*From the fullness of his grace we have all
received one blessing after another.*

JOHN 1:16

During this Christmas season,
May you be blessed
With the spirit of the season,
which is peace,
The gladness of the season,
which is hope,
And the heart of the season,
which is love.

JOHN GREENLEAF WHITTIER

Dear Heavenly Father,

Christmas is such a wonderful time of year. I love the celebrations and memories, the songs and decorations. Thank You, Lord, for giving us a time of year to simply focus on joy.

Today, Lord, may my joy be based in You, in Your gift of salvation, and may I spread that joy to others.

Amen.

Love came down at Christmas
Love all lovely, love divine.
Love was born at Christmas,
Stars and angels gave the sign.

CHRISTINA G. ROSSETTI

Comfort from on High

*When doubts filled my mind, your comfort
gave me renewed hope and cheer.*

PSALM 94:19 NLT

Part of the wonder of Christmas is the comfort that
comes to us, the way we're suddenly inspired to comfort
others. Maybe it's the snow or the gifts or the beauty of
Christmas that comforts our souls—or maybe it's the
good news of a Baby's birth, a gift of God's light into the
darkness of the world.

Christmas—that magic blanket that wraps itself
about us, that something so intangible that it
is like a fragrance. It may weave a spell of nostalgia.
Christmas may be a day of feasting, or
of prayer, but always it will be a day
of remembrance—a day in which
we think of everything we have ever loved.

AUGUSTA E. RUNDEL

Cookies from Heaven

MARGARET LANG

Nibbling on broken pieces, my daughter, Karin, decorated sugar cookies. "Not as tasty as Grammy's snowball cookies—by far," she reminded me.

"No, they aren't," I agreed. We'd sung the same forlorn tune every Christmas since my mother's passing.

How could Mom have slipped away without the recipe getting into our hands? I missed all her recipes, but especially those snowballs. During the last few blustery holiday winters, I had often daydreamed that the recipe might swirl down from heaven like a snowflake. The vision seemed so real—like I could actually see it fluttering down toward me—but of course it wasn't. I put it out of my mind.

"It would look better outside with more light strands, Mom," my son, Norm, said as he poked his snow-covered head in the door.

"Okay, I'll look for some." I walked out to the garage and after digging through a pile of Christmas supplies, I found another strand of lights at the bottom, next to a dingy box. A sweep of my hand across its dusty surface revealed a name. Wasn't that the moving company that brought items from Mom's house? Every carton from her estate had been emptied out years ago. What was that box doing here?

Temporarily forgetting the Christmas lights, I tore open the flaps. Reams of old accounting papers. Nothing interesting, which explained why I had not sorted them out years earlier.

As I replaced the contents in the container, my fingers touched something hard at the bottom. A small wooden box lay hidden there.

I opened the lid and gasped. Mom's recipes. Almost too good to be true.

I scanned the markers—hors d'oeuvres, salads, meats, potatoes, breads, sauces, candy, desserts.... My heart pounded. *Please let it be here.* Finally, at the very back, I saw it—cookies!

Smells of yesteryear bombarded my memory, and I was in olfactory bliss.

I levered out the tightly stuffed cookie recipes and looked through them, card by card, then again more carefully. Every one was there—except the sought-after snowballs recipe.

"Where is it, Lord?" I whispered.

I consoled myself with memories. As a little tyke, my hands barely reached the confectioner's sugar-covered snowballs on the counter. How I loved to lick the powdery sweetness off my fingertips.

As I got older, I realized the secret of the appeal of these little cookies wasn't the powdered sugar, but Mom's light shortbread which melted delectably in my mouth. Before she had time to work her way down the long row with the "snow," I grabbed a plain ball—or two—at the end of the assembly line. She never scolded me for the pilfered cookies.

At Mom's festive parties, guests quickly discovered that the little white cookies far surpassed all the brightly colored confections. Nobody could eat just one snowball. A gathering of twenty-five people polished off fifty—easy.

The cookies had made a wonderful tradition, that was for sure. But I had grown cold out in the garage and I was getting nowhere. I gathered up the outdoor lights for Norm and put the recipes back in the box.

Suddenly, my eye lighted on the cram-packed section of uncategorized cards at the front of the recipe box. I hadn't noticed it before. I tugged. It didn't budge. It was stuck tight.

In exasperation, I gave a big yank.

The tattered white cards broke free. They scattered up into the air, and in the dim garage, they seemed to flutter like broad paper snowflakes.

I scooped them up and moved under the light of the window. In my mom's faded script, I read "Hot Crab Spread," "Chicken Ruby," "Date Bread"—and then "Snowballs." I breathed out a long sigh.

Of course—Mom had always kept her favorite recipes together at the front of the box, I now remembered.

"Karin!" I shouted as I tripped up the stairs into the kitchen, clutching the precious oil-stained card. "Guess what? I found the snowball recipe, just like in my wildest dreams."

"No kidding!" Karin gasped as she took it from me. "Ooh, yum."

Without losing a second, she pulled out the mixing bowl and spoons. We combined all the ingredients and even double-sifted the flour for the lightest possible shortbread.

When Norm again peeked in the door from the cold, the aroma drew him inside.

Soon the oven-fresh wonders were powdered and ready to eat. Three white mustaches took shape as we contentedly enjoyed the love cookies from heaven. ✳

Every good and perfect gift is from above.

JAMES 1:17

Snowballs

1 CUP BUTTER

? CUP CONFECTIONER'S SUGAR, PLUS EXTRA FOR ROLLING

2 TEASPOONS VANILLA

1 TABLESPOON WATER

2 CUPS SIFTED FLOUR

1 CUP CHOPPED NUTS

Cream butter and sugar. Add vanilla, water, and flour and mix, then add nuts. Form into small, quarter-sized balls and bake on an ungreased cookie sheet at 300° for 20 minutes or until bottoms are slightly browned. While hot, roll in additional confectioner's sugar. Makes three dozen.

That, of course, is the message of Christmas.
We are never alone. Not when the night
is darkest, the wind coldest, the world
seemingly most indifferent.
For this is still the time God chooses.

TAYLOR CALDWELL

The Little Red Wagon

PATRICIA LORENZ

To be perfectly honest, the first month was blissful. When I moved Jeanne, age six, Julia, four, and Michael, three, from Missouri to my hometown in northern Illinois the very day of my divorce from their father, I was ecstatic to be in a place where there was no fighting or abuse.

But that first month passed quickly, and I started missing my old friends and neighbors. I missed our lovely, modern, ranch-style brick home in the suburbs of St. Louis, especially after we'd settled into the ninety-eight-year-old white frame house we'd rented, which was all my post-divorce income could afford.

In St. Louis we'd had all the comforts: a washer, dryer, dishwasher, TV, and a car. Now we had none of these. After the first month in our new home, it seemed that we'd gone from middle-class comfort to poverty-level panic.

The bedrooms upstairs in our ancient house weren't even heated, but somehow the children didn't seem to notice. The linoleum floors, cold on their little feet, simply encouraged them to dress faster in the mornings and hop into bed more speedily in the evenings.

I complained about the cold as the December wind whistled under every window and door in that old frame house. But they giggled about the "funny air places" and simply snuggled under the heavy quilts Aunt Bernadine brought over the day we moved in.

I was frantic without a TV. What would we do in the evenings without our favorite shows? I felt cheated that the kids would miss out on all the Christmas specials. But the children were more optimistic and much more creative than I. They pulled out their games and begged me to play Candyland and Old Maid with them.

We cuddled together on the gray tattered couch the landlord provided and read picture book after picture book from the public library. At their insistence we played records, sang songs, popped popcorn, created magnificent Tinker-Toy towers, and played hide-and-seek in our rambling old house. The children taught me how to have fun without a TV.

One shivering December day, just a week before Christmas, after walking the two miles home from my temporary part-time job at a catalog store, I remembered that the week's laundry had to be done that evening. I was dead tired from lifting and sorting other people's Christmas presents, and just a little bitter, knowing

I could barely afford any gifts for my own children.

As soon as I picked up the children at the babysitter's, I piled four large laundry baskets full of dirty clothes into the children's little red wagon, and the four of us headed toward the laundromat three blocks away.

Inside, we had to wait for washing machines and then for people to vacate the folding tables. So the sorting, washing, drying, and folding took a little longer than usual.

Jeanne asked, "Did you bring any raisins or crackers, Mommy?"

"No," I snapped. "We'll have supper as soon as we get home."

Michael's nose was pressed against the steamy glass window. "Look, Mommy! It's snowing! Big flakes!"

Julia added, "The street's all wet. It's snowing in the air but not on the ground!"

Their excitement only upset me more. If the cold wasn't bad enough, now we had snow and slush to contend with. I hadn't even unpacked the box with their boots and mittens yet.

At last the clean, folded laundry was stacked into the laundry baskets and placed two baskets deep in the little red wagon. It was pitch dark outside. Six-thirty already? No wonder they were hungry! We usually ate at five.

The children and I inched our way into the cold winter evening and slipped along the slushy sidewalk. Our procession of three little people, a crabby mother, and four baskets of fresh laundry in an old red wagon moved slowly as the frigid wind bit into our faces. We crossed the busy four-lane street at the crosswalk. When we reached the curb, the front wagon wheels slipped on the ice and tipped the wagon over on its side, spilling all the laundry into a slushy black puddle.

"Oh no!" I wailed. "Grab the baskets, Jeanne! Julia, hold the wagon! Get back up on the sidewalk, Michael!"

I slammed the dirty, wet clothes back into the baskets.

"I hate this!" I screamed. Angry tears spilled out of my eyes.

I hated being poor with no car and no washer or dryer. I hated the weather. I hated being the only parent responsible for three small children. And if you want to know the truth, I hated the whole blasted Christmas season.

When we reached home I unlocked the door, threw my purse across the room and stomped off to my bedroom for a good cry.

I sobbed loud enough for the children to hear. Selfishly, I wanted them to know how miserable I was. Life couldn't get any worse. The laundry was still dirty, we were all hungry and tired, and there was no supper started and no outlook for a brighter future.

When the tears finally stopped, I sat up and stared at a wooden plaque of Jesus that was hanging on the wall at the foot of my bed. I'd had that plaque since I was a small child and carried it with me to every house I'd ever lived. It showed Jesus with His arms outstretched over the earth, obviously solving the problems of the world.

I kept looking at His face, expecting a miracle. I looked and waited, and finally said aloud, "God, can't You do something to make my life better?" I desperately wanted an angel to come down on a cloud and rescue me.

But nobody came—except Julia, who peeked into my bedroom and told me in her tiniest four-year-old voice that she had set the table for supper.

I could hear six-year-old Jeanne in the living room sorting the laundry into two piles: "Really dirty, sorta clean, really dirty, sorta clean…"

Three-year-old Michael popped into my room and gave me a picture of the first snow that he had just colored.

And you know what? At that very moment I did see angels before me—not one, but three. Three little cherubs, eternally optimistic and once again pulling me from gloom and doom into the world of "Things will be better tomorrow, Mommy."

Christmas that year was magical as we surrounded ourselves with a very special kind of love, based on the joy of doing simple things together. One thing's for sure: Parenthood was never again as frightening or as depressing for me as it was the night the laundry fell out of the little red wagon. Those three angels have kept my spirits buoyed and today, thirty years later, they continue to fill my heart with the presence of God.

The Lord himself goes before you and will be with you;
he will never leave you nor forsake you.
Do not be afraid; do not be discouraged.

DEUTERONOMY 31:8

The First Noël

TRADITIONAL CAROL

The first Noël the angel did say,
Was to certain poor shepherds in fields as they lay;
In fields where they lay keeping their sheep,
On a cold winter's night that was so deep.

Noël, Noël
Noël, Noël
Born is the King of Israel

They looked up and saw a star,
Shining in the east beyond them far,
And to the earth, it gave great light,
And so it continued both day and night.

*For my eyes have seen your salvation, which you have
prepared in the sight of all people, a light for revelation
to the Gentiles and for glory to your people Israel.*

LUKE 2:30-32

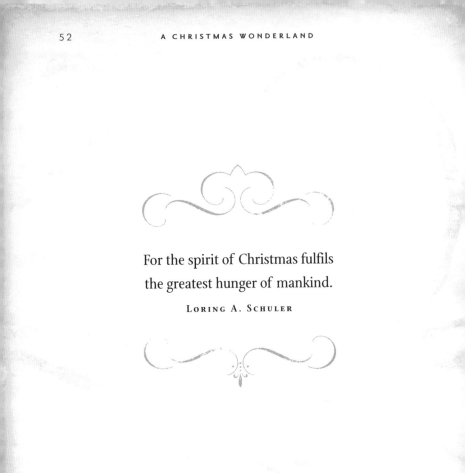

For the spirit of Christmas fulfils
the greatest hunger of mankind.

LORING A. SCHULER

At Birth

CHARLOTTE ADELSPERGER

Jesus, Son of God, was
born of a young woman;
cradled in her loving arms—
held close to her heart.

Spiritually I am a child of God,
given newness through Christ;
cradled in everlasting arms—
held always to His heart.

*As a mother comforts her child,
so will I comfort you.*

ISAIAH 66:13

Dear Heavenly Father,

Some years, the holidays are difficult, and rather than lifting my spirits, they remind me of things in my life that hurt. But, Lord, I thank You that the very reason for Christmas—the coming of Your Son to seek and save what is lost—is more than enough reason to celebrate.

Thank You, Lord, for Your comforting, loving presence in my life during the Christmas season and all year round.

Amen.

The magical dust of Christmas
glittered on the cheeks of humanity
ever so briefly, reminding us
of what is worth having and
what we were intended to be.

MAX LUCADO

The Wonder of Hope

*"For I know the plans I have for you," declares the LORD,
"plans to prosper you and not to harm you, plans
to give you hope and a future."*

JEREMIAH 29:11

There's something about Christmas that renews our
hope and reawakens our belief that things will get better.
The spirit of Christmas is a spirit of God's guiding,
helping, loving presence in our lives, a presence that gives
us a deep, joyful hope.

In the depth of winter
I finally learned that there was
in me an invincible summer.

ALBERT CAMUS

Santa's Visit

LOUISE TUCKER JONES

Just thinking about Christmas was difficult that year, not to mention shopping, decorating, baking, and pretending to enjoy the holiday. Our son, Travis, not quite three months old, had died in September, and I felt like a part of me had died with him. What kept me in the Christmas mode that year was our four-year-old son, Aaron, who had been going through his own stages of grief, but was nonetheless looking forward to Santa's visit.

I wanted to make life as normal as possible for Aaron, which meant following our usual holiday tradition of spending Christmas Eve at my parents' place with my siblings and their children. Aaron was accustomed to waking on Christmas morning at his grandparents' house to see his Santa gifts under the tree, and this year we planned to do the same.

But in spite of my good intentions, things weren't the same. There was no Christmas joy in my heart. Each time I wrapped a child's gift, I remembered the toys I had bought for Travis that would never find their way under the tree. When I looked at

Christmas stockings hanging and waiting to be filled, I noticed only the one that was missing. And since family members had no idea how to comfort me, they usually said nothing at all, which left me feeling lonely and sad.

On top of all that, relatives who usually weren't present at Christmas dropped by for a visit, making my parents' small frame house bulge at the seams. Unable to handle the laughter and the noise and the crowd, I told my husband, Carl, I wanted to go home. But I didn't really want to make that long drive back to our empty house either. We sat in the car—the only quiet spot we could find—and discussed our options.

Finally, we came up with an idea. Carl's dad, who had been a widower for several years, lived in the same town as my parents and had recently remarried. His house was empty and only fifteen minutes away. We talked with Dad by phone and he encouraged us to make use of his home. It sounded good to us.

But four-year-old Aaron wasn't convinced. "How will Santa find me?" he asked. We assured him that Santa would know where he was.

There was another problem. "But there's no Christmas tree at Pa-Pa's house," Aaron said sadly.

"Santa will bring one," we said. That was something he had

never seen happen, so he was skeptical—but also very tired. And so, finally, he agreed to go to Pa-Pa's house and climbed into bed as soon as we arrived.

After Aaron went to sleep, Carl and I looked at each other and said, "What are we going to do?" We had anticipated the lack of a Christmas tree and thought we had solved the problem. My father had cut four feet of the top of their tree in order to make it fit through the door. We had stashed the top of the tree in the trunk of our car, but we had one tiny problem: We had no decorations.

Not wasting any time, we got innovative. We popped popcorn and strung it across the little tree, and I made colorful chains from Christmas ribbon to drape from the branches. One of Dad's dresser drawers was filled with small medicine cups, which we covered with foil, adorned with curly ribbon, and tied to the tree. They looked like shiny little bells. After adding a handful of bows and a few other festive little trinkets, we stepped back from the tree, pleasantly surprised. It actually looked like a Christmas tree.

Finally, we took some wrapped packages, along with Aaron's Santa present—a complete set of dinosaurs—and spread them on a white sheet under the tree.

Aaron was more than surprised—he was shocked. He could

hardly believe his eyes when he saw the Christmas tree. Santa really did know where he was, and the dinosaurs were exactly what he wanted. I hadn't seen my son that happy in weeks. And I hadn't felt that spark of joy since Travis' death. I curled up on the sofa with a cup of coffee and watched Aaron and his daddy play with the toys, savoring the love and solitude of the moment.

I certainly cried my share of tears that holiday season. But that somewhat unconventional Christmas was a turning point in our lives. I believe God provided a sweet respite for us that morning, then presented us with a challenge. He challenged us not just with the task of decorating a tree, but the challenge to live again, to laugh, love, cry, and go on in spite of our pain.

That Christmas was the beginning of a healing time for Carl and me as we worked and laughed together for the first time in months to turn a scraggly old treetop into an eye-catching Christmas tree to surprise a little boy who was afraid he would miss Santa. That day, the three of us began the task of carrying on. ✸

I will guide him and restore comfort to him,
creating praise on the lips of the mourners in Israel.

ISAIAH 57:18-19

A Christmas Carol

G. K. CHESTERTON

The Christ-child lay on Mary's heart,
His hair was like a fire.
(O weary, weary is the world,
But here is the world's desire.)

The Christ-child stood at Mary's knee,
His hair was like a crown,
And all the flowers looked up at Him,
And all the stars looked down.

The Christ-child lay on Mary's lap
His hair was like a light.
(O weary, weary is the world,
But here is all aright.)

The Christ-child lay on Mary's breast,
His hair was like a star,
(O stern and cunning are the kings,
But here the true hearts are.)

Wait quietly.

Wait patiently.

Wait attentively.

He makes all things beautiful in His time.

ROY LESSIN

The Spirit of the Lord is on me,
because he has anointed me
to preach good news to the poor.
He has sent me to proclaim freedom for the prisoners
and recovery of sight for the blind,
to release the oppressed,
to proclaim the year of the Lord's favor.

LUKE 4:18-19

However many blessings we expect from God,
His infinite liberality will always exceed
all our wishes and our thoughts.

JOHN CALVIN

Christmas in a Refugee Camp

RENIE BURGHARDT

During World War II, my family and I had many sad Christmases. Fear and uncertainty were always lurking in some nearby corner. Those were the years we observed Christmas mainly in our hearts, with very little in the way of outward celebration. So when we arrived in the refugee camp in Austria just a few weeks before Christmas, I wasn't expecting anything different. At age eleven, I had become resigned to holidays without a lot of feasting and gifts.

The refugee camp, with its wooden barracks and dusty lanes, was pretty drab. But we had a warm place to sleep and warm food to eat and were outfitted with warm clothes donated toward the refugee effort by various generous-minded countries like the United States, Canada, and Great Britain. So we considered ourselves very fortunate. And we had some of the most beautiful scenery available, free to anyone who wished to look, since the camp was located in one of the most scenic areas of Austria-Carinthia.

As Christmas approached, the refugee camp school I attended made plans to help us celebrate the holiday as a group. In the barracks where we lived, our private spaces were tiny cubicles, occupied almost entirely by our cots for sleeping—there was no room for individual celebrations. But in the school's large auditorium, someone set up a donated Christmas tree, which the children helped decorate with our own handmade ornaments. Tiny candles perched on the tree too, waiting to be lit on Christmas Eve, just like they did before the war.

We also began rehearsing the school Christmas play, which we would present on Christmas Eve. I had a small part as the angel who comes to proclaim to the shepherds the news of the Savior's birth, and I was very pleased and excited about my upcoming acting debut.

On Christmas Eve afternoon, my grandparents and I decided to take a walk to the small town of Spittal, just a few miles from the camp. Grandfather felt that even though we had no money to buy anything, taking in the Christmas sights and smells would be worth the walk. The cobbled streets ambling among the small shops were decorated with fir branches, and small trees in shop windows glowed with lit candles. People hustled and bustled, getting last-minute items for the holiday and wishing each other "Froliche Weinachten" ("Merry Christmas").

We stopped in front of a bakery and inhaled the delicious smells that rushed forth every time someone opened the door. I gazed at the pretty, delicately layered Napoleons displayed in the window, my mouth watering. "Oh, they must taste so delicious," I said wistfully.

"And that poppy seed kalacs looks wonderful too," Grandmother sighed, referring to the sweet pastry commonly known as kuchen.

"Maybe this wasn't such a good idea," Grandfather said with sadness in his voice. "Now everyone is hungry for something they cannot have!"

"But who is to say that you cannot have a Napoleon, or some of that poppy seed kuchen?" a voice behind us asked as a woman in a fur coat and hat took my hand. "Come on, let us all go into the bakery."

"Oh, no, I couldn't possibly—" I protested, trying to pull my hand out of hers. But she wouldn't let go, and once inside the bakery, she bought a large Napoleon square and some kuchen, just for us. "Froliche Weinachten," she called out merrily, and then disappeared into a crowd of people. A Christmas angel in a fur coat.

On the way back to the refugee camp, as I sank my teeth into that delicious, custard-filled Napoleon, getting powdered sugar all over my coat, I didn't think I could get any happier. But there were even more wonderful surprises ahead.

That evening, the candles on the community Christmas tree were lit and all the adults filed into the auditorium for our Christmas play, which went off very nicely. Everyone remembered their lines and the choir sang

beautiful Hungarian Christmas songs, and by the end of the perform-
ance, our audience had tears in their eyes. Then the presents were handed
out—for, yes indeed, under that tree were presents for all the kids.

When I opened mine, I found a pair of fuzzy red mittens and a
matching scarf in the box. Inside one of the mittens was a little note,
written in English: "Merry Christmas from Mary Anne in Buffalo, New
York, United States of America." Imagine that, a gift from a girl all the
way in America! Later that night, I tried to fall asleep, my imagination
working overtime wondering how old she was, what she looked like,
what she liked to do.

When I awoke on Christmas morning, it was already light out,
and there were noises thumping through the thin wooden boards of
the barrack.

"Good morning, sweetheart. Merry Christmas," Grandmother said.

"Why is there so much noise out there already?" I asked sleepily,
rubbing my eyes.

"Well, I guess some early-rising children are enjoying all the newly
fallen snow."

"Oh, did it snow last night?" I said, leaping from the cot and
reaching for some warm clothes to put on, including my new mittens
and scarf. "Wonderful! And where is Grandfather?"

"He and some of the other men are shoveling some paths so people can go for their breakfast and to church."

Within seconds, I was out there too, marveling at nature's power to turn a drab refugee camp into a pristine winter wonderland.

Soon, the surrounding snow-covered hills were filled with Austrian children sledding down in their new Christmas sleds or on their new skis, their squeals of delight matched by those of the refugee camp children building snowmen, having snowball fights, and making snow angels. Nature's gift of snow was free for everyone to enjoy.

Later as I gazed at the snow-covered mountains with their majestic, frosted spruce trees, so breathtakingly beautiful, my heart filled with joy. Then, looking up at the sky, I thanked God with tears in my eyes for a wonderful refugee camp Christmas. ✶

You have done many good things for me,
Lord, just as you promised.

PSALM 119:65 NLT

Hark! The Herald Angels Sing

CHARLES WESLEY

Hark! the herald angels sing,

"Glory to the newborn King!

Peace on earth, and mercy mild,

God and sinners reconciled."

Joyful, all ye nations rise,

Join the triumph of the skies;

With th'angelic host proclaim,

"Christ is born in Bethlehem."

Hark! the herald angels sing,

"Glory to the newborn King!"

Christ, by highest heav'n adored;

Christ, the everlasting Lord;

Late in time behold Him come,

Offspring of the favored one.

Veiled in flesh, the Godhead see;

Hail th'incarnate Deity

Please, as man with men to dwell,

Jesus, our Immanuel!

Hark! the herald angels sing,

"Glory to the newborn King!"

Hail! the heav'n-born Prince of Peace!

Hail! the Son of Righteousness!

Light and life to all He brings,

Ris'n with healing in His wings.

Mild He lays His glory by,

Born that man no more may die;

Born to raise the sons of earth,

Born to give them second birth.

Hark! the herald angels sing,

"Glory to the newborn King!"

Dear Heavenly Father,

Every day of the year, You provide a deep, renewing, sustaining hope. You remind us that You're in control, that we have no need to fear the future. But on Christmas, that hope is even more special, because we're reminded of when hope began: when Christ came into the world.

Thank You, Lord, for the gift of Your Son and for a season of hope.

Amen.

If, instead of a gem, or even a flower,
we should cast the gift of a loving thought
into the heart of a friend, that would be
giving as the angels give.

GEORGE MACDONALD

The Gift of Love

*If we love one another, God lives in us
and his love is made complete in us.*

1 JOHN 4:12

Of course there's more to Christmas than shopping for
that perfect winter coat or that special rod and reel. But gift-
giving is a favorite tradition nonetheless. We love to anticipate
the expression on a loved one's face when we finally decide on
the perfect gift, something that perfectly expresses our love.
Maybe that's what makes Christmas gifts so special: They
reflect our love and remind us of God's love for us.

God gave us memories that
we might have roses in December.

J.M. BARRIE

The Gift of a Lifetime

LYDIA E. HARRIS

I hurried through the crowded mall, searching for last-minute Christmas gifts for my husband and children. For the last several years, my holiday shopping list had also included gifts my elderly parents wanted me to buy for their seven married children and twelve grandchildren (which meant that their gift to me was never a surprise, since I always bought it).

But this year was different. My parents hadn't said anything about gifts or asked me to shop for them. I certainly didn't mind—I had plenty of shopping of my own to do. But as I dodged life-sized nutcrackers and slow shoppers in the mall aisles, I wondered—were they too old to care about gift giving? After all, both were in their eighties, and Dad was almost ninety.

Christmas Eve arrived, and we picked up my parents for our family celebration. To my surprise, they greeted us with faces wreathed in smiles—and armloads of Christmas presents of varying shapes. "We just finished wrapping our gifts for the family," they informed us, looking like children with the excitement that blushed in their cheeks.

My parents chattered happily in the backseat of our station wagon during the half-hour drive across town. Sometimes they whispered to each other, obviously pleased with their secret. Dying of curiosity, I asked, "So what'd you get me for Christmas?" They chuckled but didn't reply. "How about a little hint?" I coaxed. But I couldn't weasel a single clue out of them.

When we arrived at my sister's house, the sage-laced smell of roast turkey welcomed us and made our stomachs growl. "Merry Christmas!" and "Good to see you!" cheerfully rang out over the ensuing flurry of hugs. We took off our coats and warmed ourselves by the crackling fire, contentedly reminded of past Christmases by the song on the stereo system: "Joy to the world, the Lord is come..."

After feasting on turkey and all the trimmings, we gathered around the tinseled tree as Dad read the Christmas story from the Bible. I noticed that he seemed more hurried than normal, not commenting on the passage as he usually did.

Then it was time to exchange gifts. Dad, usually not terrifically excited about presents, couldn't wait to begin. "Mom and I want to be the first to give our gifts," he said. "But don't open them until everyone has one." He read the names from each package as Mom handed them to the children and grandchildren.

Two generations of Siemens waited in suspense, curious about the contents of the boxes we were holding. When everyone held a present, Dad said, "Now you may open them."

Sounds of tearing paper filled the room, followed by several of us asking, "What's this?" as assorted food boxes emerged beneath the wrappings. Surely we hadn't received what the cartons proclaimed we had. We opened shredded wheat and Hi Ho cracker boxes, but did not find cereal or crackers. We each discovered the same gift—a book.

My white-haired father spoke in a quavering voice. "As I approach my ninetieth birthday, I have a strong desire to leave something behind to speak when I can't."

The thought of Dad dying added a somber quietness to the moment.

He glanced at Mother, who nodded and patted his leg in encouragement. "As I looked back on the exciting and touching experiences in our lives, I felt a deep yearning to share them with others."

I glanced down at my book, reading the title: *Heartcries and Blessings: The Reflections of a Russian-Born Servant of God* by Nicolai

Siemens, my father. Stories he had told me flashed through my mind, stories of religious persecution, imprisonment in Russia as a Mennonite minister, God's intervention, and their miraculous escape in 1929.

Dad continued, "I began to pray like Job, 'Oh that my words were printed in a book!' The printing of this book is an answer to many, many prayers." He pulled out his handkerchief and wiped away tears.

The room was silent. Completely surprised, none of us knew how to respond. We looked at our books, each carefully inscribed with a personal message. Mine read: "Lydia, your artistic talents are paying dividends at home and in the church. We love you. Your parents, Nicolai and Helen Siemens."

I glanced through the pages and saw personal stories, poems, and spiritual insights. I began reading, only half registering the recorded memories.

I was too stunned to fully appreciate their gift that Christmas. That would come later, when I could allow my heart to really remember my parents. But for now, they were alive, sitting near me, and I could talk to them in person. Two years later, they both passed away, and I saw how priceless their gift was.

Now, over a decade later, with grown children and grandchildren of my own, I treasure my surprise gift far more than I thought possible. I'm inspired by my father's courage to self-publish a book at age eighty-nine. Because Dad took the time to record stories from their lives, my family and generations yet unborn can learn about their Christian heritage. His testimony echoes the Psalmist's: "They will still bear fruit in old age, they will stay fresh and green, proclaiming, "The LORD is upright; he is my Rock" (Psalm 92:14-15).

As octogenarians, my parents weren't too old to care about gift giving. Instead, they gave a priceless gift—one that outlasted any others. ✶

A righteous man will be remembered forever.

PSALM 112:6

You can give without loving,
but you can never love without giving.

AMY CARMICHAEL

*For God so loved the world
that he gave his one and only Son,
that whoever believes in him
shall not perish but have eternal life.*

JOHN 3:16

The greatest gift
that you can give to others
is the gift of unconditional
love and acceptance.

BRIAN TRACY

The Clock

ESTHER NORTH

When my family moved to our prairie farm after World War II, there wasn't an evergreen tree in sight. So we were very excited when we learned that a shipment of fir trees would arrive from the West Coast in time for Christmas. Dad and I eagerly volunteered to hitch up the horses and go to town to choose one before they were picked over.

We stomped all around the lot in our boots as Dad picked up one tree after another, giving each one a good shake and setting aside the ones he liked. Finally, the choice came down to two that he judged had a nice, even fill of branches. We chose the taller one.

Before we could fit it into the big farmhouse living room, the stately evergreen had to lose a few branches and we had to rearrange the furniture. Mom said she would never let the two of us choose the tree again—but the next year and every year after, we laughed as she shook her head in friendly, exaggerated dismay at the size of the tree. When the tree's branches finally settled down and spread out, Mother unpacked the box of fragile glass decorations and tinsel.

The radio was playing Christmas songs, and Mom and Dad sat on the sofa holding hands and suggesting where I might hang every precious figurine and hand-painted glass ball. Once the ornaments were in place, I needed Mom's help to make sure the tin candle holders with their short white candles were secure on the branches.

Then Dad brought the ladder in to put the angel on the top branch—that was his part—and Mom whipped up a big basin of Ivory soap "snow." The three of us all spooned it onto the branches, mounding it to look like the snow on the English Christmas cards, since prairie snow is too cold to rest in mounds on tree branches.

There were only two disappointments that year.

The first disappointment was mine when I heard my dad pronounce the real candles too dangerous to stay lit. They would only be lit briefly, he said, when we came home after midnight mass on Christmas Eve for eggnog and the opening of one gift. (I always chose to open a gift that was not a surprise. Surprises were for Christmas morning.) To my delight, the next year, and for all the Christmases to come, the trees were lit by "real colored lights" powered by the tractor battery until electricity finally came to the farm.

The other disappointment was my romantic mom's. She tried to look ever so pleased, but we could tell when she unwrapped her gift from Dad that it wasn't what she had hoped for. The dry paper around the gift gave way to the biggest blue, enameled roasting pan any of us had ever seen, just what was needed for the homegrown turkey stuffed and ready for roasting—but not what was needed to delight Mom's heart.

The following year, remembering Mom's disappointment and determined not to make the same mistake the next year, Dad enlisted my help. I don't remember what I said, but I'm sure I was very subtle about it—casually mentioning to my mother what I wanted for Christmas and, by the way, what did she want Santa to bring her?

Dad and I went shopping for Mom's gift on the day we went to choose the Christmas tree. We were just deciding on a prettily boxed set of Tweed parfum de toilette and talc when we heard the clock chime.

It was a Westminster chime clock, and the pharmacist had wound it up for customers to hear. The chimes sounded to me like romantic, faraway places, and Dad said his mother had had a mantle clock much like it. And so, even though it exceeded the budget, we agreed that the beautiful oak clock was perfect, and arranged for it to be held at the store until Christmas Eve—it had to be a surprise.

When Christmas Eve finally came, Mom, Dad, and I traveled into town by open sled, waving good wishes to all our neighbors as the harness bells rang. Dad dropped Mom and me off at the grocery store, giving me a quick wink to confirm that, according to our prearranged plan, he would conceal the clock in the sled while Mother was busy.

Later, we began our journey home, the light of the moon and stars sparkling on the snow. The sled box was lined with sweet smelling hay for warmth and comfort, and I imagined Baby Jesus as warmly snuggled in with His mother as I was with mine. We chattered happily for a while, then settled into the sleepy comfort of singing carols and retelling stories.

We were almost home when Mom shushed us. "Listen! What was that?"

From under the blankets and straw came the muffled but unmistakable chimes of Westminster. The sled's vibrations had started the clock.

"Just harness bells," said Dad, shooting me an anxious look.

"No, it's ... it's a chiming clock." After a moment's hesitation, like a herald angel, she proclaimed, "What a beautiful sound!"

We knew the jig was up. When we got home, we unloaded the sleigh and bedded the horses, and then, hot drinks in hand, we watched as Mom unwrapped and admired the clock. Dad wound it, set it to the minute, and started the chimes—that Christmas Eve and every week for the rest of his life.

We both said how sorry we were that her surprise was spoiled. She insisted that she wasn't sorry at all and that it would be the beginning of a new tradition to wake up to our own Westminster chimes on Christmas morning.

The next day, Dad surprised both of us.

The last gift under the tree, the one that even I didn't know was there, was the Tweed parfum and talc set. Mom cried and said, "You shouldn't have."

Dad replied, "Don't want you smelling like milking cows all the time," as he planted a kiss on her forehead.

My mother was right about the clock beginning a new tradition in the family: Their grandson now takes the key out of the little door on the back of the clock, opens the convex glass door that protects the face, and winds it up each week to keep time for his own daughters.

It was more than a clock: It was a symbol of love, a love that flooded our little farmhouse that day and continues to flood the lives of my family, on through the generations. And as the clock chimes each Christmas Eve, the love will resound and echo in our hearts for years to come. ✷

Let love and faithfulness never leave you;
bind them around your neck,
write them on the tablet of your heart.

PROVERBS 3:3

The magi, as you know,
were wise men—wonderfully
wise men who brought gifts
to the Babe in the manger.
They invented the art
of giving Christmas presents.

O. HENRY

A Christmas shopper's complaint
is one of long-standing.

ANONYMOUS

How to Give a Spectacular Christmas Gift

BRUCE KARAS AS TOLD TO SUSAN KARAS

My wife, Sue, and I recently celebrated our twenty-eighth wedding anniversary. Over the years, we've had plenty of good times together, as well as our share of spats and disagreements. But we're pretty good about compromising when necessary.

Except, unfortunately, when it comes to Christmas shopping.

"What do you want for Christmas this year?" I'll ask hopefully.

"Surprise me," she'll answer—two words that strike fear in my heart.

"So...don't you want to know what I want?" I inquire next, thinking longingly of a particular fishing rod or DVD.

"Don't you worry about it—I've got a few ideas up my sleeve," she answers coyly with a peck on my cheek.

The conversation ends there. And there lies our problem.

I had clues right from the start that gift-giving would be a sore spot in our relationship. Sue could never comprehend my family's gift-giving habits at all. My family delights in asking, "What is it?"

before we open a gift, half expecting an answer. The element of surprise factors in very little in our shopping—and that drives Sue absolutely nuts.

"What's the fun of wrapping a gift if you all are going to pick it up, feel the weight, shake it, and then guess what it is before you open it?" She frowns and continues, "I can't understand it. Don't you like surprises?"

"Well, come on, Sue—your family's just as nuts. The way they go on and on about how much they love their gift—'Oh, a hundred thanks, it's just perfect.' A simple thank you is sufficient. Oh, and I don't need to know why they chose the gift or where they shopped for it."

"Well, fine," she says curtly, stomping out of the room.

"Fine," I answer, just to have the last word.

And so the Christmas gift rigmarole has gone through the years. Sometimes I start praying at Thanksgiving, *Lord, get us through the Yuletide season peacefully.* And sometimes we have. Other times, however, have been a disaster, with Sue in tears because I got her an electric mixer or a crock pot.

Women! Why do they want something romantic? Give them something they need, I always say. And then she gets mad because

I don't surprise her.

Or, even worse, I don't like her surprise to me.

"You never like anything I get you! Doesn't matter what it is," she complains. But I can't help it if I don't like cashmere sweaters or fancy watches.

Why can't she just do it my way? It's so much easier. Just pick any item from my illustrated and annotated wish list. And please, provide the same for me, with size and color preference clearly denoted, thank you very much.

Then, one Christmas, some accidental eavesdropping on my part saved us.

I had come home early one day, unexpectedly, and walked in to hear my wife chatting on the phone. "No, I'm not even shopping for Bruce this year! I think I've finally learned. He wants something out of the West Marine catalog. He left the ad by the coffee pot.... Yeah, highlighted and everything. Not subtle at all. But that's okay; I can still go to the mall for my other gifts. I just decided to give him a gift he really wants this year."

I pumped a fist—I was getting my top-of-the-line Penn rod and reel.

My joy was short lived. Now I had to come up with a surprise for her—right? She was finally doing what I'd wanted all these years, and now I had to return the favor. How was I going to pull this off?

That night at dinner, I plied gently, "Honey, what do you want for Christmas this year?"

She handed me a Macy's ad. "I want this handbag."

She was going to do it my way this year?

"They go on sale this Sunday."

Even better! But, interestingly, rather than being thrilled to finally get to do Christmas shopping the way I wanted, I was suddenly touched by her change of heart. Now I was even more determined to give her the Christmas surprise of her life.

She interrupted my thoughts. "Hey, we've got be at Donna and Joe's by 8:00."

"Why? What's going on?"

"They're having a karaoke party." Her eyes sparkled.

Sue loves karaoke. And Donna and Joe have an awesome setup, complete with professional microphones and hundreds of songs to choose from. And they always put out a great spread too. Tonight would be great, as always—we'd kick back and enjoy an evening with friends. I'd worry about the gift dilemma later.

Everyone had fun visiting and laughing and, of course, singing. And in the spirit of *Star Search* and *American Idol*, we jokingly declared a tie between Joe's "Delilah" and Sue's rendition of "Crazy."

We left in high spirits, with hugs and "Happy holidays" to all.

That night, as Sue slept soundly and I lay awake with Journey songs ringing in my head, it hit me—the perfect gift, the perfect surprise. I slipped quietly out of bed and tiptoed into our den. I logged onto the Internet and began my search, and in no time flat, I was done. It would be delivered to a friend's house so Sue would never know.

The week before Christmas was a flurry of activity as all of us scrambled to get our last-minute shopping done and get the gifts wrapped and arranged under the tree. On Christmas Eve, we baked Christmas cookies and sang carols—and I slipped away to call my friend. He would drop Sue's gift off early Christmas morning on the way to his mom's place. I'd already wrapped the handbag she wanted, but it was only a decoy. All systems were go on Operation: Surprise Sue.

When Christmas morning finally came, I was more anxious than a six-year-old. I couldn't wait to surprise my wife. We had a huge breakfast, then moved into the front room, where we sat around the glittering tree and opened our gifts amid the usual oohs and ahhs. Everyone was happy with their presents, especially me. I proudly held the oh-so-perfect rod and reel in casting position and shot Sue an appreciative smile. She held up her handbag and smiled right back.

Afterward, she looked around at the sea of discarded wrapping paper, bows, and ribbons. "Well, guess that's it. Merry Christmas, everyone! We'd better get this mess cleaned up."

"Not quite yet." I opened the door to the garage and lugged in a huge box. "One more gift here. For you, Sue." Funny, I suddenly felt nervous. What if she didn't like it?

Her eyes grew wide. "For me? Are you kidding?"

"Go on, open it!"

"Yeah, open it, Mom," the kids said in unison, in on my surprise.

She tore off the Santa paper and red ribbon and just stared in amazement. Then she almost cried. "My very own karaoke system, just like Donna and Joe's! Now we can host karaoke parties too, and I can practice any time I want."

I felt like I was on top of the world as I saw excitement and pleasure play across her face.

"Thanks, hon, this is the best gift you ever gave me!" She threw her arms around my neck and hugged me tight.

This was definitely the best Christmas we'd ever had—not because we both got what we wanted, but because we both learned a different way to give. ✴

God loves a cheerful giver.

2 Corinthians 9:7

Dear Heavenly Father,

Today, Lord, may I not be caught up in shopping, but in giving. May I not be focused on giving extravagantly to win the favor of others, but on giving to encourage their hearts. May each gift I give reflect the heart of the world's greatest Giver.

Amen.

A joy that's shared is a joy made double.

ENGLISH PROVERB

Family and Friends

Love one another deeply, from the heart.

1 PETER 1:22

When we recall our favorite Christmas memories, what we remember most are our loved ones. Christmas just wouldn't be Christmas without brothers and sisters to share inside jokes with, parents to bake cookies with, or grandparents to swap stories with. We don't experience the warmth of the season until we're sharing it with someone we love.

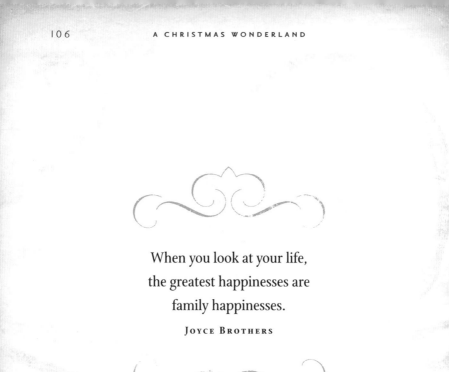

When you look at your life,
the greatest happinesses are
family happinesses.

JOYCE BROTHERS

Chocolate Kisses Before Breakfast

JEAN STEWART

It's 5:00 a.m. on Christmas morning. I slip quietly out of bed and down the stairs, turn on the tree lights, and sit in the soft Christmas glow. Digging into my stocking, my fingers find a foil-wrapped drop of chocolate. I unwrap it and let it melt on my tongue. The semi-darkness and velvety sweetness of the chocolate plunge me back to my childhood.

One particular, chilly Christmas morning, an eerie light fell across the walls of my room as my little brother cracked open the door. He stared at me until I squirmed awake.

"Hey."

"Has he come?" I whispered.

"Yep."

"You sure?" My nine years to his four gave me authority.

He nodded and grinned, motioning for me to hurry.

I crawled out from under the warm covers and ignored the cold oak floor beneath my bare feet as I followed him, heart racing with anticipation, into the living room. The lights on the spruce

Christmas tree softly cast the walls and floor in red light. We searched the floor under the lowest branches, afraid to hope yet filled with excitement for what Santa may have left there.

Steve's eyes grew huge with delight as he reached for a red fire truck, large enough to sit on, its dazzling shine reflecting the tree lights. I gazed at the most beautiful doll in the world, her long-lashed eyes blinking with each nod of her head, her perfect curls bouncing past her waist. I pulled her onto my lap and my eyes roamed the room. They stopped at two stuffed and overflowing red stockings propped on Daddy's big armchair. We had no fireplace, no mantel, but that didn't deter Santa. Steve and I grabbed for the fuzzy socks at the same moment.

Oversized red apples and tangerines were in the toes, small toys and games filled the spaces between the heel and the hem, and nuts and candy canes poured out of the tops. But the object of our search was the chocolate. Our fingers wrapped around the little pyramid-shaped candies, and we tore off the foil and popped them in our mouths. We didn't chew. Not yet. The first ones had to melt and cling to the roofs of our mouths.

My brother's closed-mouth smile mirrored my own as the sun rose and tried to break through the cold, gray Georgia morning.

The white bisque Virgin Mary smiled down at her infant Son from her position of honor opposite the tree, and we played with our new treasures while the rest of the family slept. It would be hours before grandparents, aunts, uncles, and cousins arrived and breakfast was served. We were content on the floor with our toys and our yearly early-morning chocolate treat.

It was Christmas.

Now, so many years later, I sit quietly reflecting. Soon the silver dawn calm will be broken by squeals, strewn paper, and the chug and whistle of an electric train, while the aromas of baking cinnamon buns and country ham, apple cider, and freshly ground coffee will mingle with the evergreen crispness and fill the air. Our children will get into their stockings and find their own chocolates and my husband and I will relive our own time of innocence through them. For now, though, I am alone.

I think of my brother and imagine that we're sharing this quiet, sleepy time, 3,000 miles apart. I picture him as he holds the candy in his mouth in the glow of his own tree and remembers with me. Just for a little while, if only in my heart, we are together as the chocolate melts.

The jingle of the telephone breaks into my reverie. Maybe it's him. As I race toward the insistent ringing, I feel a childlike hope.

"Hey."

The sound of his voice makes the morning right. I'm transported to the simplicity of those mornings spent sitting on the floor with my little brother, sharing chocolate kisses before breakfast.

And now it's Christmas. ✳

Love is what binds us all together in perfect harmony.

COLOSSIANS 3:14

Light of the World

NANETTE THORSEN-SNIPES

There's a light in your eyes
That reminds me of
The Light of the world,
especially at Christmas.

There's a smile in your voice
When you sing carols
About the King of Kings
And Lord of Lords.

There's a warmth in your hugs
That feels as if God carries me
Close to His heart during
This season of His infinite love—

The love that lights the world.

Glorify the LORD with me; let us exalt his name together.

PSALM 34:3

I have always thought of Christmas time
as a good time; a kind, forgiving, charitable,
pleasant time; the only time I know
of in the long calendar of the year,
when men and women seem by one
consent to open their shut-up hearts freely.

CHARLES DICKENS

The Too-Tall Christmas Tree

PEGGY FREZON

Daylight was fading as we pulled into the Christmas tree lot. Maybe it would be closed, I hoped silently. But the festive white lights strung across the entrance were still lit.

Usually, I couldn't wait to get our tree and decorate it with Mike and the kids. I loved the big, old-fashioned lights, the hand-me-down glass ornaments, and the sparkling silver tinsel we always hung one strand at a time. At night, we'd turn off all the lights in the house and sit around the tree, mesmerized by the twinkling colors. Even my teenage kids hadn't grown too old to enjoy the spirit of this simple holiday tradition.

But this year, the cherished tradition didn't seem so simple. It wasn't that I didn't want a tree. It was just, well, the size. My husband insists that a proper Christmas tree must at least skim the ceiling. Our snug, older house is far from large, but the ceilings are more than ten feet high. And a ten-foot high tree tends to get pretty bushy, with branches that easily take over an entire living room.

"Maybe we could try a smaller tree this year," I lightly

suggested as everyone tumbled out of the van. Thoughts of a simple little evergreen on a table in a corner filled my mind.

A man with tan coveralls and thick boots approached. "Could you point us toward the Frasier Firs?" Mike asked, and then added, "The big ones?" My heart sank.

The man led the way to a row of fragrant firs leaning against a rough wooden frame. "Here's a real big one," he said, grasping a tree with his heavy gloves. Mike stretched his arm up to gauge the height and smiled. He couldn't even reach the top.

"It looks a little, um, tall..." I began.

I tried desperately to point everyone toward the more reasonably sized pines in the front. But before I knew it, they were admiring the tree with that look on their faces. I just looked up and up—and up.

"Wait! It's too tall!" I said, Scrooge-like.

The kids' rosy faces beamed. Mike glowed with satisfaction. The coveralled man waited expectantly for an answer. I didn't have the heart to cause a fuss.

At home, Mike dragged the tree into the kitchen, and I gasped as branches compressed and squeezed through the slender doorframe. Where on earth were we going to put this Redwood?

In the past we'd tried various different locations, but the huge bushy greenery was always in the way of something. And somehow it seemed each year's tree topped the one the year before. I scowled at the inconvenience Mike's tree was causing.

"I could try rearranging the furniture," Mike offered. He moved a chair out onto the porch, then dragged the loveseat, couch, and coffee table against the far wall. He tugged the enormous fir into the newly freed corner. It looked like we were on the Titanic and all the furniture had slid to one end. Only instead of an iceberg, a monstrous tree loomed before us.

It looked awful. I pouted like a child who found coal in her stocking. Angry words were on the tip of my tongue. "I told you so!" I wanted to say. "I told you not to get a big tree! I told you it wouldn't fit!" But I stopped myself suddenly.

The mood was as icy as the frigid winter weather outside. I was feeling anything but jolly and bright. The kids had scattered to avoid the fall-out. And Mike—Mike looked like a man who was trying to provide his family with a Christmas tree the best way he knew. I read the disappointment in his eyes.

I knew without a doubt that what happened next was totally in my control. I could react in anger and spew out those hateful words—"I told you so"—or I could ignore the minor inconveniences and rejoice in the grandeur of the grand fir. Was the size of the tree important enough to ruin Christmas?

I took a deep breath and surveyed the space again. I felt the tenseness in my muscles relax. "How about if we try it over there?" I pointed.

"It'll be in the way," Mike warned softly.

"That's okay," I nodded.

"We'll have to shove the dining table up against the wall."

I was silent for a moment. "I can live with that," I said finally.

When all the pushing and pulling was done, our ten-and-a-half-foot tree stood in the back of the dining room, branches jutting out crazily every which way. Although it took up half the room, the tree was elegant and beautifully proportioned. A Christmassy aroma filled the room.

It took us all night and fifteen strings of big, old-fashioned bulbs to fill up that tree. Hundreds of special ornaments adorned the boughs. Mike placed our old cloth angel at the top, and she looked down, reminding me of a central focus I had forgotten. How silly of me to have overlooked the more important meaning of Christmas.

That night, the whole family snuggled in the dark, admiring the colorful lights, hand-blown glass ornaments, and glittery tinsel. It didn't matter that the furniture was cramped to one side or that we constantly banged our heads on the dangling light fixture once protected by the placement of the table. My family was sharing a special moment together, once again mesmerized by the twinkling colors. No, it didn't matter if it was big or small, tucked neatly in the corner or inconveniently placed. Our Christmas tree was way too tall, yet that night I knew it was simply perfect. ✳

Love one another. As I have loved you,
so you must love one another.

JOHN 13:34

It is not flesh and blood
but the heart which makes
us fathers and sons.

JOHANN SCHILLER

Forever Sisters

NANETTE THORSEN-SNIPES

It was springtime, and azaleas and dogwoods bloomed throughout Atlanta, flooding the grounds of South Fulton Hospital. But that beauty didn't live in my heart. My mother was near death and my sisters and I were at odds.

After Mama's funeral, my sisters and I went separate ways and lost touch after a couple of years. Both sisters moved several times, while my stakes remained rooted in northeast Atlanta. I heard from my middle sister periodically through birthday cards and phone calls, but I completely lost touch with my youngest sister.

Retta's pretty face and blonde, wispy hair deceived most people. She could out-scrap any boy, and was forever getting into some kind of trouble. When she was six, I gave her a small white Bible and wrote her name inside, hoping it would help keep her on the straight and narrow. But when she hit her teens, "trouble" became her middle name, and I guess I gave up.

As the years passed, I missed my sister terribly. When we

parted, I had four children, the youngest only four years old, while Retta's only child was entering first grade. During the intervening years, my former husband committed suicide, and my father nearly died, ending up in a veteran's home. My family went through birthdays, Christmas, Easter, and other holidays without ever hearing from Retta.

Though I wanted to find my sister, I gave up trying after ten years and finally released her to God's care.

Years later, I stood on a chair taping Christmas cards to a doorframe when I saw the postman put another handful of cards into our mailbox. I stepped down and finished placing the nativity scene on top of the television. My thoughts turned to the first Christmas, and as I placed the tiny baby between Mary and Joseph, I reflected on Jesus, God's love-gift to the world. And at that moment, I deeply wished I could share that love with my younger sister.

Wrapping my bulky gray sweater around me, I stepped into the biting cold to retrieve the mail. I noticed every card had a return address—all except one bright red one. Curious and excited, I flipped it over and opened it.

"Please forgive me, Nan," the familiar handwriting said, "I

apologize for not getting in touch sooner. I hope we can talk." I looked at the enclosed photos and wiped away tears that quickened down my cheek. Seventeen years was a long time.

Later, when I finally talked to Retta on the phone, I learned about her husband's accident, which crushed every bone in his face and nearly killed him.

"Nan," she said, "I had no one. I didn't know anyone to call." Her voice broke, and then she regained composure. During the blackest hour of her life, my sister was totally alone. As she sat in the hospital holding a Bible, she reflected on all the years she had faced trouble alone—without her sisters. It took three months, but her husband pulled through, and they eventually resumed their lives.

I saw Retta for the first time since our mother's funeral when her twin grandchildren were born. She hadn't changed much, only gotten older—like me. My husband and I drove to the other side of Atlanta and got there just in time to take photos of her squalling grandchildren who—just like us—will be forever sisters.

Before we parted ways, Retta opened a yellowed and worn box, which held a small white Bible. She turned to the front page, where thirty-eight years before, I had written her name inside. "All those years," she mused, her voice wavering, "I thought I was alone, but I really wasn't." ✶

[Love] always protects, always trusts,
always hopes, always perseveres.

1 CORINTHIANS 13:7

Time was with most of us, when Christmas Day,
encircling all our limited world like a magic ring,
left nothing out for us to miss or seek; bound
together all our home enjoyments, affections,
}and hopes; grouped everything and
everyone round the Christ.

CHARLES DICKENS

Dear Heavenly Father,

One of the things I like most about Christmas is seeing people I don't get to see that often and taking time to celebrate together when we might otherwise be focused on the busyness and humdrum of life. Lord, I know that relationships are a gift from You, that You have created us to love others and be loved.

Today, Lord God, I pray that you would magnify and multiply the love in my life. Draw me and my family and friends closer together and help us reflect and embrace Your love.

Amen.

Never worry about the size
of your Christmas tree.
In the eyes of children,
they are all thirty feet tall.

Larry Wilde

Through a Child's Eyes

*From the lips of children and infants
you have ordained praise.*

PSALM 8:2

It's been said many times before that Christmas is
for children. Kids anticipate Christmas more excitedly
and enjoy it more deeply. It would seem that the simple
joys, the sheer magic of the season, are best enjoyed
when experienced through a child's eyes and with a
childlike heart.

Our hearts grow tender
with childhood memories
and love of kindred,
and we are better
throughout the year
for having, in spirit,
become a child again
at Christmas-time.

LAURA INGALLS WILDER

Santa Sighting

LANITA BRADLEY BOYD

"I'm staying up to see Santa this year!" I stoutly insisted, and my parents consented with surprisingly few objections. Nine years old and certain that I had the Santa thing figured out, I planned to catch my parents in the act this year.

My five-year-old brother, Larry, and I slept in an attic room only accessible by a drop-down stairway. We staged a Santa stakeout, making a pallet at the head of the stairs so we could peer down into the hallway that led to the living room. I talked Larry into lying there with me to watch, but of course he immediately fell asleep.

Soon, my own eyelids began to droop, only to spring open when I heard a noise at the front door—sleigh bells, unmistakably. Then I heard a stomping of boots, a thumping in the living room which had to be the sound of gift boxes being unloaded and stacked. I lay frozen with astonishment. As I carefully leaned forward to get a peek, I saw a large, white-haired, red-suited man, the classic Santa, standing there in my own living room. I stared, wide-eyed, as he took a step in my direction and gave a brief salute. "Merry Christmas, boys!" he chuckled, then turned and slipped out the door.

When I could no longer hear the sleigh bells, reason asserted itself, and I shot down the stairs and into my parents' bedroom, flipping the light switch and crying, "Aha! Where's Daddy?"

My sleepy-eyed dad rolled over, sat up, and said, "What's wrong? Why are you up?"

I stopped in shock. There under the covers were both my parents, asleep as usual. Then who was the red-suited man?

"You'd better get back to bed, young lady," he said. "You don't want to be up when Santa comes!"

"Oh, but he's already been here!" I cried, breathless. "I saw him! But he called us boys. You don't think he just left boy things, do you?"

"I don't know and at this point I don't care," Daddy said, uncharacteristically gruff. "I need my sleep!"

"Wait—" Mother sat up. "Did you actually see him, Lanita?"

"Yes! In the living room! And I heard his sleigh bells!" I answered, quivering with excitement.

"How wonderful!" Mother replied. "In all my childhood I

never got to see him when he came. I always fell asleep. How exciting for you, darling!"

"Well, I guess it is," Dad grudgingly agreed. "But we still need to get some sleep. You'd better scurry back upstairs, Lanita. You can't look until morning."

So I went back up to my cozy pallet and snuggled up to my warm little brother, peacefully missing all the excitement. I trembled in awe at what I'd seen—and that it had not been my dad. Amazing!

When I was eighteen, I asked my mother who had come dressed as Santa that night. She gave me a blank stare. "What are you talking about?" she said. "It was the real Santa!"

And to this day, when I am sixty and she is eighty-two, she still gives me the same answer. ✳

And whoever welcomes a little child
like this in my name welcomes me.

Matthew 18:5

There's nothing sadder in this world
than to awake Christmas
morning and not be a child.

ERMA BOMBECK

God's Presence

TONYA RUIZ

I turned on the light and reached for the ringing phone on my nightstand.

"Hello?"

"Tonya, it's Mom. Sorry to wake you up so early, honey, but I wanted to let you know that Grandpa died."

I hauled my huge pregnant body out of my warm bed, waddled into the living room, and plugged in the lights on the Christmas tree. As I looked at the brightly wrapped presents, my eyes filled with tears. I wondered how I would tell my three little children that their precious Papa died on Christmas Eve. Poor Papa, he had been blind for years, but he loved rocking my Zachary and listening to Ashley and Lindsay sing.

After breakfast, I told the kids, "Last night Papa moved to heaven." For the rest of the day, it was hard for any of us to be joyful. My six-year-old busy bee, Ashley, tried to take her mind off her loss by making her bed and cleaning up her room. My five-year-old, Lindsay, snuggled close to me, holding onto her blankie and sobbing, "I already miss my Papa."

"Presents, Mommy!" Zachary said gleefully, shaking one of the gift boxes under the tree.

"Stop playing with those gifts!" I scolded him for the zillionth time. Then I foolishly tried to reason with a two-year-old. "Sweetie, I know you're excited and it's hard to be patient, and you've been waiting for a long time, but you can't shake the presents or rip the paper off of them yet." Zachary crinkled up his nose, smiled, and then began taking the candy cane ornaments off the tree and putting them into a pile. *I give up*, I thought. *I'm already exhausted and it's only eight o'clock in the morning.*

Later that day at my parents' house, I asked my folks if they thought we should cancel our Christmas party. But Mom had already decided the matter. "Papa wouldn't want the kids to miss out, so let's just do what we'd planned," she said firmly.

That evening, my brother, sister, nieces, and nephews all piled into my parents' house. The adults tried to put on happy faces as the children joyfully decorated the lopsided gingerbread house with frosting and gumdrops. Finally, it was time to open gifts. My girls immediately ran to a bedroom to try on their new dress-up clothes, and Zachary's chubby little hands unwrapped toys, toys, and more toys.

The next morning, with logs burning in our fireplace, my husband, Ron, read the Christmas story from the Gospel of Matthew. Then we let the children tear the paper off their brightly wrapped presents and eat candy from their stockings. That afternoon, for the grand finale, we bundled the kids in their jackets and drove to visit my husband's brother. Zachary was ecstatic when he realized there were more colorfully wrapped gifts waiting underneath their tree.

Sadly, the following day, we all gathered in a little white chapel for my grandfather's funeral. Holding onto my husband's arm, I waddled in with my little ones following like ducklings. We filed into the wooden pew and little Zachary was sitting by my side. As the organist finished playing "Amazing Grace," I opened my purse and began searching for tissue.

The gray-haired pastor stood up behind the pulpit and began to pray. "Lord, we thank You for Your presence here today—"

As soon as he heard the word "presence," mistaking it for its homophone, Zachary jumped up on the pew, stretched out his arms, and with a smile from ear to ear, yelled, "Presents, yay! More presents!"

Everyone laughed and turned to see the noisy culprit, whom I was gently wrestling onto my lap. The pastor looked over at me, winked, and said, "Actually, the little guy has a point. I wish everyone was that excited about God's presence. Maybe we've all learned a good lesson today. God's presence really is a present."

I leaned down, kissed Zachary's little cheek, and whispered, "I love you" into his ear.   He nuzzled his face into my neck and fell asleep looking quite angelic. ✶

In Your presence is fullness of joy.

PSALM 16:11 NKJV

At that time Jesus said, "I praise you, Father,
Lord of heaven and earth, because you have hidden
these things from the wise and learned, and
revealed them to little children. Yes, Father,
for this was your good pleasure."

MATTHEW 11:25-26

Kids: They dance before they learn
there is anything that isn't music.

WILLIAM STAFFORD

Away in a Manger

J. C. FILE AND JOHN T. MCFARLAND

Away in a manger, no crib for a bed,
The little Lord Jesus laid down His sweet head.
The stars in the sky looked down where He lay,
The little Lord Jesus, asleep on the hay.

The cattle are lowing, the Baby awakes,
But little Lord Jesus, no crying He makes;
I love Thee, Lord Jesus, look down from the sky
And stay by my cradle till morning is nigh.

Be near me, Lord Jesus, I ask Thee to stay
Close by me forever, and love me, I pray;
Bless all the dear children in Thy tender care,
And fit us for Heaven to live with Thee there.

It is good to be
a child sometimes,
and never better
than at Christmas,
when its mighty Founder
was a child Himself.

CHARLES DICKENS

The best of all gifts
around any Christmas tree:
the presence of a happy family
all wrapped up in each other.

BURTON HILLIS

Wrapped with Love— and Lots of Tape

PEGGY FREZON

Mike and I were busy gift-givers that year—shopping, wrapping, and hiding gifts under the tree three weeks before Christmas. Our four-year-old son, Andy, watched closely as we pulled the rolls of colorful paper from the hall closet and carefully tied ribbons and bows. Sometimes he helped operate the tape dispenser, covering gifts with more sticky stuff than paper.

He watched, too, as we wheeled through the stores, carefully selecting just the right sweater for Uncle Randy, the perfect coloring set for his cousin Crystal. "What's dat?" he'd ask, and I'd explain about the pretty dishes for Gramma or the special book for his sister, Kate.

"Me, too," he'd say. I always thought he meant he wanted a present, too.

On Christmas morning, I found out otherwise.

As everyone was gathered around the tree, excitedly ripping paper and exclaiming over new clothes and CDs and toys, Andy reached under the tree and withdrew a handful of gifts.

"Here, Mommy," he said, plunking down in my lap and handing me a present. I recognized the zealously-taped wrapping as his style.

"What could it be?" I asked. Mike hadn't mentioned taking him to the store to buy me anything. I pulled off the holly-green paper to reveal a fork. Just like one of the forks in our kitchen drawer. In fact, it was one of the forks from our kitchen drawer. I looked at Andy's face, expectant and proud.

"Why, thank you, Andy! It's just what I wanted!" I laughed, giving him a huge hug. He looked up at me, beaming with happiness. He jumped up and handed out the rest of his presents.

Mike worked at his well-sealed gift to discover the garage key dangling from its glowing orange chain. "I was wondering where this went," he whispered to me before turning to Andy and exclaiming, "It's perfect!"

Kate unwrapped a small, well-used blue plastic pony with a rainbow-colored tail. "Thank you, Andy," she smiled, playing along. She gave her brother a big hug.

There were other surprises, too: a deck of cards, a pen, a tape measure. Andy looked like he'd just given us all a million dollars.

And the funny thing was that we felt the same way.

I don't know when he did it, or how he managed to do it in secret. All I know is he wanted to be a part of Christmas that year. And he was—thanks to Andy, that Christmas we all saw that the spirit of giving is all wrapped up in the heart, even if it comes wrapped with half a roll of tape. ✶

God loves the person who gives cheerfully.

2 CORINTHIANS 9:7 NLT

Dear Heavenly Father,

Thank You, Lord, for Your love for children. Thank You for the joy they add to any holiday, for their bright spirits and joyful hearts. Most of all, thank You that You call us Your children and invite us to experience life as Your sons and daughters. Today, please lighten our burdens and help us experience the holiday with childlike faith and gratitude.

Amen.

The joy of brightening other lives,
bearing each other's burdens,
easing other's loads, and supplanting
empty hearts and lives
with generous gifts becomes
for us the magic of Christmas.

AUTHOR UNKNOWN

Tidings of Joy

But the angel said to them, "Do not be afraid.
I bring you good news of great joy
that will be for all the people."

LUKE 2:10

When the shepherds first heard about the Baby Jesus,
they rushed to see Him. And when they saw Him, they
rejoiced, exulting in God's power and presence. Now,
many years later, when we celebrate Christmas, we
celebrate the same good news that brings us great joy.

Those who bring sunshine
to the lives of others cannot
keep it from themselves.

JAMES MATTHEW BARRIE

Laura's Christmas Surprise

ANNE CULBREATH WATKINS

"What in the world?"

My husband, Allen, and I stared at the brightly decorated Christmas tree standing in the living room. I just hadn't been motivated to set it up last week like I'd planned, and it certainly hadn't been there when we went to bed the night before. Our astonished eyes gaped at the big piles of beautifully wrapped gifts waiting beneath it, and the Christmas stockings that dangled from hangers nearby. "Laura must have done all this when she came in from work last night," I guessed.

Like a couple of excited kids, the two of us prowled around under the tree, picking up and shaking each gift. "I never heard a thing," Allen said. "Did you?"

"Not a sound," I replied. Our daughter, Laura, worked second shift and I always made sure to listen for her car in the drive each night. But somehow, I hadn't heard our Christmas elf come in that night, much less create a mini-wonderland.

Favorite family Christmas decorations were hung around the

living room, and strings of colorful lights blinked cheerily on the tree. Each gift bore a tag filled out in Laura's distinctive handwriting, sweet messages scrawled on several. How she managed to set up the tree and wrap all those gifts without waking either of us mystified me. Unexpected delight filled my heart, and I wondered if this was how Laura felt at Christmastime when she was growing up.

I had always tried to make Christmas special for her, often going to extreme lengths to get the things she put on her wish list. One year, it was a nearly impossible to find purple bicycle with unicorn decals. Another time, it was a roller skating stuffed dog with long blonde ears that matched Laura's hair. And each Christmas morning, the delighted expressions on her bright, beaming face made all the trouble worthwhile.

Somewhere along the way, though, I stopped looking forward to the holidays. Hard years of financial difficulties, several family deaths, and bouts of depression dimmed my Christmas joy. I struggled to work up enthusiasm and holiday cheer, but it never seemed to work, and I greeted each holiday season with a dullness of spirit that kept me from enjoying much of anything.

I didn't want to decorate the house or go shopping for gifts, and putting up the tree was a chore I put off as long each year as possible. Many times, I prayed for the strength to get through the holidays and maybe even to enjoy them, but somehow it seemed as though my prayers never got any further than the ceiling.

But now, I stood in my living room, completely overwhelmed by the sudden appearance of this Rockefeller-worthy tree and the piles of gifts heaped beneath. A bit of the choking depression melted away as the warmth of Laura's thoughtfulness took hold. For the first time in years, I realized that I was looking forward to Christmas morning.

The big day took its time in arriving, and on Christmas morning we excitedly tore into the piles of presents. I found everything from the wish list Laura had insisted I give her, along with a few special surprises. A lovely black handbag, a silver jewelry box, and one of my favorite movies emerged from the cheery gift wrap. There was even a box of thirty diskettes. And she hadn't forgotten Allen, either.

Standing just shy of six-foot-four, he can be difficult to buy clothing for, but somehow Laura managed to find two pairs of blue jeans in just the right size. "Go try them on," she urged excitedly. Allen gave her a bear hug, then disappeared down the hall with the pants. Laura and I happily examined our gifts as we waited.

Finally, Allen strode into the living room, clad in a T-shirt and a pair of the new jeans. "Look!" he commanded.

Laura and I glanced up, admired the jeans, and resumed our chattering. "No," Allen cried, gesturing dramatically toward the floor. "Look!"

We stared at his feet, then burst into laughter. One hem dragged the floor, the other hit somewhere above his ankle. "Honey, they'll be fine," I managed to gasp, "as long as you stand sideways on a hill!"

As we dissolved into hysterical giggles, Laura ran for the camera and snapped a few shots of Allen modeling his mismatched hems. The last little bit of ice melted from my heart and I brushed tears of joy and laughter from my eyes. The sadness of the past vanished as Laura's Christmas surprise brought me the joy I couldn't find on my own. Through her actions, God's love uplifted my broken spirit and restored the joy of the season to my heart. ✳

You have filled my heart with greater joy
than when their grain and new wine abound.

PSALM 4:7

Where children pure and happy
Pray to the blessed Child,
Where Misery cries out to Thee,
Son of the Mother mild.
Where Charity stands watching,
And Faith holds wide the door,
The dark night wakes, the glory breaks,
And Christmas comes once more.

FROM "O LITTLE TOWN OF BETHLEHEM"
BY PHILLIPS BROOKS

Come and see what God has done,
how awesome his works in man's behalf!

PSALM 66:5

Christmas Everywhere

PHILLIPS BROOKS

Everywhere, everywhere, Christmas tonight!
Christmas in lands of the fir-tree and pine,
Christmas in lands of the palm-tree and vine,
Christmas where snow peaks stand solemn and white,
Christmas where cornfields stand sunny and bright.
Everywhere, everywhere, Christmas tonight!

Christmas where children are hopeful and gay,
Christmas where old men are patient and gray,
Christmas where peace, like a dove in his flight,
Broods o'er brave men in the thick of the fight;
Everywhere, everywhere, Christmas tonight!

For the Christ-child who comes is the Master of all,
No palace too great, no cottage too small.

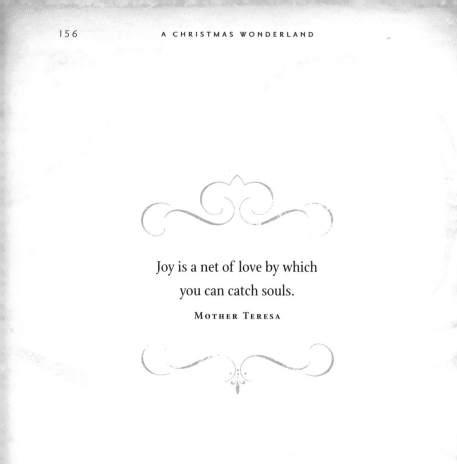

Joy is a net of love by which
you can catch souls.

MOTHER TERESA

The Perfect Gift

LANE CLAYTON AS TOLD TO JOAN CLAYTON

Christmas was almost here, and my daughter, Kallie, desperately wanted a soccer Beanie Baby. She wanted it so badly that my wife and I, being the generous (and peace-loving) parents that we are, gave in and presented her with the Beanie Baby early. From that point forward, she slept with it, ate with it, and took it everywhere she went.

The week before Christmas, it was my turn to serve communion to the elderly members of our church who can't make it to the services. Kallie went with me, clinging to her new favorite toy as had been her practice the last couple weeks.

The first person on our list was George, a kindly old gentleman who lived in a nursing home not too far away. I had visited George before and always enjoyed it. He was fun to talk to, and sometimes I even forgot how old he was. When we walked into his room, he seemed happier than usual to see us. Kallie, who is really good with the elderly, immediately walked over and gave him a big hug. The smile on his face seemed to grow from the depths of his heart. There's nothing quite like the love of a little child to brighten anyone's day.

I asked George if he had any family around for the holiday. He simply said no. I asked him how he had been doing, and he replied, "Not very well." He elaborated by saying that he just wasn't having a good day. But I was impressed with his attitude about it. He seemed to know that God was in control, but that we all have to accept the good with the bad. As I glanced over to my daughter, I could see the sympathy in her eyes. It was the kind of sympathy that only a child can have in their somewhat limited understanding of an adult world, a pure kind of sympathy that knows no age boundaries.

Our conversation wound down, and Kallie and I served George communion. And then we started saying our goodbyes. Just as he did the last time I visited him, George got up and said he would walk us out, saying it was good for him to get up and walk around from time to time. When we exited the building, he kept on walking through the courtyard with us, right to the gate out by the street. I shook his hand and thanked him for walking us out. Seeming truly grateful to have had visitors, he thanked us for coming.

And then my daughter completely surprised me. As she went to hug him goodbye, she held up her Beanie Baby and said, "You can have it." I found myself wanting to interject and say, "No—

you don't have to..." but I couldn't speak. George tearfully and silently bent down to accept the hug—and the Beanie Baby.

Those few seconds are frozen in my mind. I can see the smile on his face and the look of compassion in her eyes. My mind was trying to comprehend what I had just witnessed. My eight-year-old daughter had just shown me Christ in action. Her love and compassion was a natural and immediate manifestation of her love and obedience. What self-sacrifice! I can only hope and pray that I could be so loving and giving.

As we made our way to my truck, I turned and looked back at George. My lasting memory, burned into my mind forever, was that of a bent-over old man, who had just been touched with God's comfort and joy through the heart of a little child, shuffling back to his confinement, clutching a little smiley-faced plush toy.

I put the truck in drive and, eyes watering, told my daughter that I loved her and that I was proud of her and that she had just made God smile. ✶

Carry each other's burdens, and in this way
you will fulfill the law of Christ.

GALATIANS 6:2

From "God Rest Ye Merry Gentlemen"

ENGLISH, TRADITIONAL

God rest ye merry, gentlemen, let nothing you dismay,
Remember Christ our Savior was born on Christmas Day;
To save us all from Satan's power when we were gone astray.

O tidings of comfort and joy, comfort and joy;
O tidings of comfort and joy.

From God our heavenly Father a blessed angel came;
And unto certain shepherds brought tidings of the same;
How that in Bethlehem was born the Son of God by name.

O tidings of comfort and joy, comfort and joy;
O tidings of comfort and joy.

The shepherds at those tidings rejoiced much in mind,
And left their flocks a-feeding in tempest, storm and wind,
And went to Bethl'em straightaway this blessed Babe to find.

O tidings of comfort and joy, comfort and joy;
O tidings of comfort and joy.

Then the angel said to them,
"Do not be afraid, for behold,
I bring you good tidings
of great joy which will
be to all people."

LUKE 2:10

Dear Heavenly Father,

You have filled my heart with great joy, Lord. Thank You for the many blessings You've poured into my life, for the beauty of Christmas and for the beauty of Your Son. Lord God, today I choose to think on the good things in my life and pour my heart out in gratitude to You.

Amen.

Christmas is a piece of one's home
that one carries in one's heart.

FREYA STARK

Home for Christmas

*For where two or three come together
in my name, there am I with them.*

MATTHEW 18:20

Whether "home" is miles away or right next door, filled with family or filled with friends who feel like family, it's the only place to be for Christmas. Home brings back childhood Christmas memories and brings us back to the people we love. Home is familiar and safe. And home reawakens our sense of comfort and joy.

Perhaps the best Yuletide decoration
is being wreathed in smiles.

AUTHOR UNKNOWN

The Christmas Tree

SARAH OLIVER

There were pine needles everywhere—on the couch, on the floor, down my shirt, and in my hair. Not to mention all over Richard's head, which was at the moment buried underneath the tree trying to figure out why it kept flopping over onto our couch instead of standing up in the tree stand.

We bought this cantankerous tree because it was Christmas—and not just any Christmas, but our first Christmas together. We weren't going to be at our apartment on Christmas morning, but I still felt like we needed a tree to get us in the spirit in the weeks before the big day. Plus, my parents have this great photo of my dad sawing the end off their first Christmas tree. He is beaming, smiling proudly at my mom, who is holding the camera. I always looked forward to having a similar moment with my husband on our first Christmas.

Two hours into our first Christmas tree moment, I am caught between the wall of our living room and a volatile pine tree. It could strike again at any moment, poking my face with its sharp needles while at the same time hurling several others onto our already littered carpet. That tree was fighting me, I was sure of it. One look at my shiny new Ikea furnishings and it wanted to bolt out the door. I was trying to hold it steady from behind while Richard sawed, twisted, and pushed, hoping to secure it into the tree stand. The tree refused to go in, insisting instead on throwing itself around the room and infuriating my husband.

I could have seen it coming. The way things had worked out for us so far should have lowered the bar on my expectations. But I am a stubborn idealist. I always have been. I expect the smiling husband in the photograph and everything that it suggests: a painless first attempt at Christmas, two completely different people coming together flawlessly, and a tree that practically walks into its tree stand and decorates itself in sheer delight at the privilege of being a Christmas tree.

I'd traveled to England to volunteer with a homeless project two and half years ago. Richard worked for the church that ran the project. We met my first day in the UK and haven't really looked back since. At the end of the summer, I returned to the States to finish my last year in college while he stayed in England to complete his Master's. We talked every day, e-mailed, wrote letters, and visited every six weeks or so. It was better than a smiling photograph; it was a fairy tale.

He slipped an antique ring on my important finger a year later. We were going to ride off into the sunset, I was sure of it.

But the Department of Immigration and Naturalisation Services turned into the Office of Homeland Security after 9/11. It was an administrative nightmare of backlogged visa applications, new rules, and busy signals. On Christmas Eve the previous year, I sat in the guest room of my parent's house on the phone with my best friend as he told me that after months of research, preparation, and prayers, he had been denied a visa into the United States. He could not be guaranteed entry for our January wedding. We had been expecting to get married and live in America.

Four weeks later, I was boarding a one-way flight to England, dragging half of my belongings with me. The other half arrived shortly after with my family, who were coming over for the wedding.

The tree thing was partially my fault. This being my first Christmas in England, not to mention my first Christmas away from my family, I needed it to feel as much like home as possible. And, in light of the previous Christmas's major disappointment, I was determined to have the smiling photograph.

Of course I wanted to forge ahead on the new frontier of many Christmases to come in the Oliver household, create new traditions, be positive and find exciting adventure in every hard situation—et cetera, et cetera—but when I saw several Christmas trees in pots at the local garden store, they did not look exciting or adventurous. Christmas trees in pots looked simply alien. Christmas trees go in stands with nice "skirts" to hide their unbecomingly knotty trunks. They sparkle and glow and touch the ceiling and take up the whole living room. Why would Richard want a small Christmas tree in a pot that barely comes up to his waist and needs to be put on a desk to look remotely substantial?

I'd forgotten he was English. I forget that a lot, considering that I live in England and hear his accent every day. I get frustrated when he comes up with strange phrases and ideas for how to do things and find it exasperating when he argues diplomatically. Aren't you supposed to wrestle through things with your gloves off?

In any case, he never forgets I am American. That's why we have this crazy Christmas tree throwing needles all over our flat:

because he remembered that I am an American having my first English Christmas away from my family. He remembers that last Christmas I lost a lot of hopes and dreams, and he wants to make it feel as close to normal as possible.

He is definitely not smiling; in fact, he looks ready to throw the freakishly tall, unpotted Christmas tree out the window. I am not going to get my smiling photo, but I have something much better. I have a husband who loves me and who, for the past two hours, has been battling with a particularly rebellious tree just to make me feel at home this Christmas. ✱

And the most important piece of clothing you must wear is love. Love is what binds us all together in perfect harmony.

COLOSSIANS 3:14 NLT

From "Being Dad on Christmas Eve"

EDGAR A. GUEST

They've hung their stockings up with care,

And I am in my old arm chair,

And mother's busy dragging out

The parcels hidden all about.

Within a corner, gaunt to see,

There stands a barren Christmas tree,

But soon upon its branches green

A burst of splendor will be seen.

And when the busy tongues grow still,

That now are wagging with a will

Above me as I sit and rest,

I shall be at my happiest.

The greatest joy man can receive

Is being Dad on Christmas Eve.

*I thank my God
every time I remember you.*

PHILIPPIANS 1:3

For centuries men have kept
an appointment with Christmas.
Christmas means fellowship,
feasting, giving and receiving,
a time of good cheer, home.

W. J . RONALD TUCKER

The Christmas I Grew Up

TERRENCE CONKLIN

It was 4 A.M. on Christmas Eve. My father was lying in my parents' bedroom with his cardiothoracic leggings on, his heart pillow to his chest for when he coughed, wrapped in four or five blankets to keep him warm. He was recovering from surgery after his recent heart attack.

My little brother was sleeping on the couch and waiting for Santa to come. He hoped to "catch him in the act" this year. This was hardly unusual for this particular night of the year, if you overlooked the fact that downstairs, two other creatures were stirring—my mother and myself.

With my father laid up after his brush with death, my mother was left to handle Christmas all by herself. And at thirteen, I was hit with the hard truth about Santa Claus.

Everything seemed completely wrong and unfair. I watched my mother wrapping last-minute gifts, placing on the tags, and carrying them up the stairs in exhaustion—of course, tiptoeing past my sleeping brother.

This had not exactly been what I had in mind for my Christmas break. I was the usual selfish teenager, who had spent the last week doing nothing but trying to get out of holiday chores. After all, I was supposed to be on vacation!

As if all of that weren't bad enough, that night I was dragged to the holiday services at church. But as I watched my mother, face on, from my position in the youth group choir loft, something changed. I saw her in our familiar pew, sitting there without my father. She was struggling to keep my brother from wiggling. She closed her eyes in a deep prayer, and tears began to flow down her cheeks. And in that moment, as if for the first time ever, I heard the commandment: "Honor your father and your mother so that you will live a long time in the land that the Lord your God is going to give you."

That night my mother and I stayed up into the wee hours of the morning, stuffing stockings, filling the empty space under the tree, and trying not to trigger the train set that now encircled the tree stand and wake my sleeping brother.

Seeing how much my mother put into Christmas with an out-of-work, desperately ill husband and two young children, made me begin to respect her. I rushed to do anything she asked, and did not grumble in my cranky, "teenage" way.

I wanted to honor both of my parents, always, and I would try to teach my brother to do the same. Especially when "Mrs. Claus" needed help.

The Christmas lights shone on my mother's face as we placed the last gift under the tree. But that Christmas I received a greater gift: I had learned honor and obedience, and I hoped we would all live long in the Lord. ✶

Honor your father and your mother, so that you may live long in the land the LORD your God is giving you.

EXODUS 20:12

Twelve Ways to Make Christmas Memories

LETTIE KIRKPATRICK BURRESS

Most of us want our holidays to be special times when we make wonderful memories with our families and friends as we celebrate the birth of Jesus. There are ways to keep things simple and still find an extravagant delight in the celebration of season. Here are a few ideas.

- Purchase an advent calendar and open a window each day.
- Keep a basket of Christmas music close by and create the mood while baking, wrapping, and decorating.
- Burn candles and fragrant potpourri throughout the season.
- Keep incoming Christmas cards in a decorative basket and pray for those families and relationships whose lives touch yours.
- Draw names in the family and become secret angels. Reveal yourselves on Christmas Eve.
- Gather weekly around an advent wreath. Light candles, read scripture, and sing carols while discussing different aspects of the Christmas story.

- Set out a basket of Christmas books containing beautiful pictures and stories related to the holiday season.
- Put only gifts for others under the tree until closer to Christmas, which will help keep the focus on giving.
- Encourage secret or spontaneous acts of kindness throughout the season. Take goodies to a service provider (pharmacist, hair stylist, owner of a favorite restaurant or grocer) with a note of appreciation. Let school children choose a needy classmate to receive an anonymous gift.
- Plan several projects focused on reaching out and meeting needs, like giving to a mission offering or to local ministries. Operation Christmas Child sponsored by Franklin Graham and Samaritan's Purse is something the whole family can get into.
- Plan a family night out and take in some light extravaganzas or a nativity reenactment. Or, plan a family night "in" and watch Christmas movies or make s'mores.
- Make a toy nativity set available so little ones can recreate their own version of the Christmas story. ✶

Dear Heavenly Father,

Thank You for setting the lonely in families. Thank You for people who care about us. And thank You for coming alongside us when we're not sure where we fit. God, I pray that You would permeate our home this Christmas. May the peace and joy of the season brighten our home, meals, and conversations.

Amen.

There is no real religious experience
that does not express itself in charity.

C.H. DODD

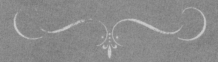

It Is Better to Give

It is more blessed to give than to receive.

ACTS 20:35

There is a wonderful sense of peace and contentment that we experience at Christmas. But again and again, in our own lives and through the examples of others, we've seen that our holiday peace and joy are deepened when we look for a way to share them with others.

The heart of the giver makes
the gift dear and precious.

MARTIN LUTHER KING, JR.

Apple Pies and Silver Dollars

C. GRANT ENDICOTT

We called my grandmother on my mother's side Mamaw. She lived just down the hollow from our house, which meant I could count on her soft arms catching me in a hug just about every day. My grandfather, Papa, was a preacher, and when I was seven he left Mamaw for a woman in his congregation. I don't remember much about the incident except that Mamaw cried a lot.

She never received any financial support from Papa. She lived on a social security check of about $400 each month. I honestly don't know how she survived—she probably wouldn't have, except for the help of my family.

I loved spending the night at Mamaw's house. She always lovingly laid handmade quilts on the bed, and on especially cold winter nights, she piled on so many that I could hardly move. At bedtime, Mamaw read from her Bible, and then she prayed. I remember noticing that her prayers weren't the kind of elaborate orations I heard at church; rather, she prayed as if she were talking to her closest friend. It seemed as if the Lord were sitting on the bed next to her. Sometimes I peeked to see if He, in fact, was sitting on the puffy white quilt.

So many things about Mamaw have inscribed themselves on my memory: the way she blessed the food as she put it away, instead of blessing it at dinnertime; those thick-cut, floury biscuits she always made; the way her kitchen smelled of apple pies from Thanksgiving through Christmas.

Getting together to bake pies was a family tradition, a holiday event in our house. The pies were wonderful—entirely homemade. Mamaw cooked the apples until they were sweet and smooth and had the consistency of apple butter. She then mixed, kneaded, and rolled the dough for the crust, lined the pans with it, and poured the apples into the shells, artfully laying thin strips of dough on top.

I still can picture Mamaw and Mother with homemade aprons tied around their waists, up to their elbows in baking flour, scraps of pie dough all over the table. They made dozens of pies, and we ate them throughout the holidays. This was part of Mamaw's special Christmas gift to all of us.

The second part of our Christmas gift from Mamaw came on Christmas Eve when all the family gathered at her house to exchange gifts. Each year, all of the children sat in a semicircle in front of the tree as we opened one gift at a time. Our last gift was from Mamaw. She came to each of us, kissed us on the cheek, told us that she loved us, and placed in our hands a matchbox, wrapped in beautiful Christmas paper. We never rushed to open the gift because we already knew what was tucked into the matchbox: a shiny silver dollar.

A silver dollar, wrapped in tissue paper, did not mean much to an eight- or nine-year-old—though Mamaw's gifts mean a great deal to me today. In a jar at home, I have twenty-two of my own silver dollars and seventeen that once belonged to my brother Bobby, who died when I was thirteen.

But as kids, what could we do with a silver dollar? We couldn't buy anything with it. It was of no real monetary value. I remember one year leaving my box unopened and playing with my toys. Mom, knowing that there would be a time in our lives when we would understand that this small gift was priceless, saved them for us in a jar in her closet.

With the gift of a silver dollar, Mamaw taught us something important about Christmas and about life, though I didn't know it at the time. Christmas was not about toys and games, but about love. It was about giving with no expectation of receiving anything in return. It was about family.

And those silver dollars taught me that the most important thing about Christmas was following the example of the greatest Giver: Whenever I think about that silver dollar, wrapped in paper, lying in a simple matchbox, I am reminded of how God gave His Son, wrapped in flesh, lying in a simple manger. And, just as that silver dollar represented Mamaw's love for me, Jesus represented God's love for the world.

Many years ago, Mamaw went to be with the Lord. Now, as fall winds turn colder and Christmas trees begin appearing in store windows, I long for the smell of those apple pies. My heart is softened as, in my mind's eye, Mamaw comes from her bedroom holding a dish filled with tiny boxes. And I say prayers of thanks for the weight and security of my family's love.

To be sure, I received some truly great gifts during the Christmases of my childhood, but the ones closest to my heart are those that came wrapped in a matchbox by a loving grandmother. ✷

*And now these three remain: faith, hope,
and love. But the greatest of these is love.*

1 CORINTHIANS 13:13

Though heralded with naught of fear,
Or outward sign or show;
Though only to the inward ear
It whispers soft and low;
Though dropping, as the manna fell,
Unseen, yet from above,
Noiseless as dew-fall, heed it well,—
Thy Father's call of love!

JOHN GREENLEAF WHITTIER

Christmas is the season
for kindling the fire
of hospitality in the hall,
the genial flame
of charity in the heart.

WASHINGTON IRVING

Turkeys, Coffee, and Transformation

LEE WARREN

I'm a thirty-nine-year-old single guy, and I often spend my weekends hanging out with two other single guys in coffee shops or catching a movie or doing a Bible study. We're like a family, and for years we've traded Christmas presents and had our own holiday celebrations apart from all our other family get-togethers.

For the past few years, we've conducted our annual gift exchange in a steakhouse—truly a guy's Christmas, I guess. We order an appetizer followed by salads and a nice, big, juicy steak dinner, and proceed to get so stuffed we can hardly move. Then we exchange gifts and nod our approval as we open another calendar or sweatshirt or baseball cap depicting our favorite sports teams. (Single guys aren't exactly known for being gifted shoppers, and we certainly are no exception.)

One of the guys in our group really—and I mean really—doesn't like to shop for Christmas presents. He says he never knows what to buy, and he often exhibits physical symptoms of stress from the process. I've never really understood his anxiety, since we buy each other the same things every year, but rather than see a friend get so distressed, I started thinking that I'd prefer to just enjoy a nice steak dinner together and skip the gift exchange. The less complicated we can make Christmas, the better, in my opinion.

A couple of years ago, as I was about to suggest to the group that we just forget about gifts and enjoy each other's company, I had an idea. A couple of days prior, I had been driving to work when I heard on the radio a plea from a local rescue mission—they desperately needed turkeys, coffee, and various other necessities. It reminded me of years past when the three of us and another friend used to buy groceries and take them to the mission during the holidays. We'd never done it in place of giving gifts to each other, but something about the idea of giving without receiving really appealed to me.

So that night, I proposed that we each contribute twenty dollars that would ordinarily go toward buying gifts for each other and use it to buy as many turkeys and as much coffee as we could for the mission. My friends loved the idea.

And so, a couple weeks later, we met at a grocery store and piled our cart full of turkeys and coffee. We spent more than the designated amount, but none of us seemed to care. The excitement we felt about giving a gift that would actually help somebody far overshadowed the fact that we had only planned to spend sixty dollars.

As we left the parking lot of the mission, we felt an overwhelming sense that these were the best gifts we'd ever given. We didn't fret about whether those who would receive the gifts would really like them or not, for surely hungry people savor hot turkey and a steaming cup of coffee more than those who have plenty of food and drink. And we didn't wonder if our gifts would be put to good use or not, because we knew that the mission was struggling to come up with enough food to feed everybody who entered their dining hall. It was a perfect Christmas gift.

Turkey shopping together has since become our new Christmas tradition. We start looking forward to it in November, and each year, we are amazed at how God uses three single guys to meet the deeply-felt needs of other people. And as a bonus, we're amazed that He would somehow use our experience to teach us the transforming power of sacrificial giving. ✳

A generous man will prosper;
he who refreshes others will himself be refreshed.

PROVERBS 11:25

You give but little when you
give of your possessions.
It is when you give of yourself
that you truly give.

KAHLIL GIBRAN

Gifts from the Heart

KAREN MAJORIS-GARRISON

It was the perfect cold, clear winter night to look at Christmas lights. "Hurry, kids!" I shouted upstairs. "Daddy's already outside warming the van."

Within minutes I heard excited voices. "Mama!" my six-year-old daughter, Abigail, shouted, sliding on her behind down the carpeted stairs. "Is the hot chocolate ready?"

"It's in the van," I told her, smiling as my two-year-old son, Simeon, tugged at my shirt.

We were all attired in our pajamas. As was our annual tradition, we all got into our sleepwear, packed a bag full of munchies, and headed into our van to look at decorations on neighboring houses.

We had just stepped out of the door when Abigail surprised me by asking, "Mama, can you give me more money for doing my chores? I want to buy you, Daddy, and Simeon the best gifts for Christmas!"

"Well, honey, the best gifts are those that come from the heart." I smiled fondly remembering the picture of a rainbow she'd drawn for me the day before when she found out I'd been feeling under the weather. "Do you remember that Bible verse from church this morning?"

She soberly quoted Acts 20:35: "It is more blessed to give than to receive."

I kissed the top of her head, and once we were all settled into the van, we opened the bag of goodies. The kids cheered aloud as we passed by numerous homes adorned with Christmas splendor.

It began snowing lightly when we rounded the familiar neighborhood where my husband, Jeff, and I had lived years ago.

"You lived there?" Abigail asked, pointing to a newly renovated two-story house. "Why'd you move?"

I answered her many questions as Jeff turned the van onto Reeves Drive and the headlights flashed onto the first brick home of the street. The house appeared disturbingly dark compared to the bright lights displayed by its neighbors.

"The people who live there must not like Christmas," Abigail noted from the back seat.

"Actually, honey," my husband said, stopping the van briefly along the curb, "they used to have the best decorated house in the neighborhood. An elderly couple lived there. They loved Jesus very much and loved Christmas. Mommy and I used to visit them when we lived nearby." Jeff pointed to the reflective letters on the mailbox. "Looks like she still lives there."

He clasped my hand and I sighed, remembering Lena and her husband and how they used to painstakingly assemble the Nativity on their lawn. "It's mostly for the children," they'd often say. "We like to imagine them in the back seat of their parents' cars. Their little faces full of Christmas wonder as they looked at the miracle of the Baby Jesus."

"Why don't they decorate it anymore?" Abigail asked, bringing my attention to the present.

"Well," I began, remembering the dark days when Lena's husband had been hospitalized, "her husband died a few years ago, and Lena's very old. She only has one child and he's a soldier living far away."

"Tell me what she's like," Abigail said, and for the next few minutes, Jeff and I filled her in on the kind things Lena used to do. "And every Sunday after church, she'd make homemade cookies and invite us over. She's an incredible person."

"Can we visit her now?"

Simeon met Abigail's question with enthusiastic agreement, and I shared our children's excitement. Both Jeff and I looked down at our attire.

"I knew this would happen one day," he said, rubbing his forehead. "First I let you talk me into wearing pajamas in the van, and now you're going to want me to actually go visiting, right?"

I kissed his cheek and an hour later, after leaving Lena's home, Abigail and Simeon clutched the crocheted cross ornaments she'd graciously given them. "I wish I had a gift for her," Abigail said, waving at the elderly woman standing in her doorway.

The next morning, my children busied themselves upstairs on an unknown mission. After rummaging through drawers, closets, and toy chests, they descended the stairs wearing toy construction hats, snow boots, and Simeon's play tool belts.

"What is all this?" I laughed. "Are you going to fix things around here?"

"Nope," Abigail smiled brightly. "This is our gift to Lena. Since she's too old and doesn't have anyone to do it for her, we're going to decorate her house for Christmas!"

Her words brought tears to my eyes. "That's a wonderful idea," I said, calling their father. "But I think you'll need Daddy and me to help. Is that okay?"

"Sure!" they replied.

And hours later, standing with Lena on her sidewalk, we looked at our handiwork. The lights we had found in her basement were shining with pride over snow-capped arches and windows. Candy canes lined the sidewalk and welcomed passersby to the Nativity scene that Abigail and Simeon had positioned on the snow-covered lawn.

It had been a day full of hard work, but it was worth every second to see the elation on Lena's face. She disappeared inside her home and returned carrying a tray of freshly baked cookies.

Abigail reached her hand inside my coat pocket and clutched my fingers. "This was fun, Mama. It really is better to give than to receive," she said contentedly.

I turned to my husband, proud of our daughter. Our eyes met and he smiled. "Looks like we've got a new Christmas tradition," he announced, and the kids heartily agreed. ✶

Since God chose you to be the holy people whom he loves, you must clothe yourselves with tenderhearted mercy, kindness, humility, gentleness, and patience.

COLOSSIANS 3:12 NLT

Dear Heavenly Father,

When I was in deep need materially or emotionally, You sent someone to help me along. And when I was in deep need of saving, You sent Your Son to save me. Lord, thank You for always lavishing me with Your grace and goodness. Today, Lord, I recognize that giving is even better than receiving, and I pray that You would use me to meet the needs of others.

Amen.

God grant you the light
in Christmas, which is faith;
the warmth of Christmas,
which is love; the all
of Christmas, which is Christ.

WILDA ENGLISH

The Reason for the Season

Thanks be to God for his indescribable gift!

2 CORINTHIANS 9:15

During the Christmas season, we're hard at work at the business of celebrating, giving, and sharing, which either fills us with joy or leaves us feeling weary and ragged. Our celebration is incomplete until we pause to recognize and reflect on the reason for the peace, joy, and hope of the season: God's amazing gift of His Son Jesus Christ.

Many merry Christmases,
friendships, great accumulation
of cheerful recollections,
affection on earth, and
Heaven at last for all of us.

CHARLES DICKENS

Christmas Crumbs

BEVERLY BUSH SMITH

It's 4:45 P.M. on Christmas Day. The phone interrupts the silence at our house.

"Mom?" our son David says. "Brigida just fell asleep—really late for her nap. There was just so much going on .... So we're running a little late."

They were due here at five. I take a deep breath and ask, "Can you give me a rough ETA?"

"Six," he says.

"Right."

I stand, staring at the phone after I've hung up. *Oh, Lord, we get the remains of the day. The crumbs.*

That's the way it feels, anyway. My son, daughter-in-law, Trina, and granddaughter, Brigida, have already had Christmas Eve with her family, a frenzy of gifts and cookies and kisses for eleven adults and six kids. And an Italian feast. And this morning, they've joined the same group for Christmas brunch. By the time the three partygoers reach us, they'll all be exhausted and cranky.

And they are. I'd thought we'd open Christmas presents first, have dinner, then let Trina open her birthday presents, since today is also her birthday.

But Trina says eighteen-month-old Brigida needs to eat now—and, pregnant with their second child, she hints that she does too.

The Rock Cornish game hens I've smoked for an earlier dinner lie on hold in the oven, and the salads are ready to serve, but I still need to stir-fry the vegetables. I hastily pull off some hen meat for Brigida and begin heating the wok and getting water on the table. Cheese. Yes, that will help. I put out a wedge of cheddar to tide them over.

When at last we're seated, I say grace over our plates. My prayer somehow lacks passion.

But the dinner is good, and Brigida leaves the table to explore, returning with various parts of the crèche. Most of all, she's captivated by the baby Jesus, and her sweet, soft voice cooing "Ba-bee!" is like a balm to my frazzled mind.

"Baby Jesus," I say each time she brings the Babe to the table.

I begin to relax.

We take an intermission before dessert to open Christmas presents. Brigida is entranced with her new interactive pound-the-ball-into-the-castle-turrets toy. (See? I knew we should have opened presents first.)

Trina admires her ice cream birthday cake with the red Christmas roses, oohs over her gifts, and begins to unwind over decaf.

Dave leans back, smiling.

And Brigida happily pounds away.

It's only after they leave, as I load the dishwasher, that God speaks to my heart. It's going to be like this every year, He gently reminds me. No, I can't compete with Trina's exuberant family celebration. Yes, sometimes I feel a little slighted. But I can offer them a place of peace, and I can celebrate our peace-filled time together.

The Babe that Brigida still grasps in her tiny hand knew about peace. Jesus told His disciples, "Peace I leave with you; my peace I give you" (John 14:27 NLT). His birth gave us all the precious gift of a peaceful heart.

Brigida had it right. This day is about "the Ba-bee," our bringer of peace. ✳

Grace and peace to you from God
our Father and the Lord Jesus Christ.

1 CORINTHIANS 1:3

A Christmas Poem

VIOLET NESDOLY

This is a poem about the last page,
    about feeling panicked,
    about lists.
This is a poem about shopping and tired feet,
    about choosing the right card
    and signing your name forty-seven times.
A poem about wrapping paper, tape, and ribbon,
    about putting up lights and garland,
    bells and wreaths while playing old records.
About finding Mom's recipe
    and buying real butter for the first time all year.
This is a poem about feasting.
This is a poem about finally getting around
    to reading the familiar story and wondering,
How did something that started out so simple
    get to be so complicated?

This is a poem about hearing the songs
    of the baby Jesus—at the mall
    and having the urge to sing them to all your neighbors.
This is a poem about the magic
    of blinking lights, toy trains
    and a cup of warm cocoa.
The Holy Family coming to your cul-de-sac.
This is a poem of when home is the only place to be
    even if the tree is small, the gifts few
    and your house is crowded as a Bethlehem street.
This is a poem about candlelight and sweet carols
    in a place where simple gowns and sequin crowns
    transform even urchins and scamps
    into shepherds, angels, and wise men.
This is a poem about Christmas.

In the Bleak Midwinter

CHRISTINA ROSSETTI

In the bleak midwinter, frosty wind made moan,
Earth stood hard as iron, water like a stone;
Snow had fallen, snow on snow, snow on snow,
In the bleak midwinter, long ago.

Our God, heaven cannot hold Him, nor earth sustain;
Heaven and earth shall flee away when He comes to reign.
In the bleak midwinter a stable place sufficed
The Lord God Almighty, Jesus Christ.

Angels and archangels may have gathered there,
Cherubim and seraphim thronged the air;
But His mother only, in her maiden bliss,
Worshipped the beloved with a kiss.

What can I give Him, poor as I am?
If I were a shepherd, I would bring a lamb;
If I were a Wise Man, I would do my part;
Yet what I can I give Him: give my heart.

Late on a sleepy, star-spangled night,
those angels peeled back the sky
just like you would tear open
a sparkling Christmas present.
Then, with light and joy pouring
out of Heaven like water through
a broken dam, they began to shout
and sing the message that baby Jesus
had been born. The world had a Saviour!
The angels called it "Good News," and it was.

LARRY LIBBY

For to us a child is born,
to us a son is given,
and the government will be on his shoulders.
And he will be called
Wonderful Counselor, Mighty God,
Everlasting Father, Prince of Peace.

ISAIAH 9:6

Let us remember that the Christmas heart
is a giving heart a wide open heart that thinks
of others first. The birth of the baby Jesus
stands as the most significant event in all history,
because it has meant the pouring into a sick world
of the healing medicine of love which has transformed
all manner of hearts for almost two thousand years.
Underneath all the bulging bundles
lies this beating Christmas heart.

GEORGE MATTHEW ADAMS

This is Christmas: not the tinsel,
not the giving and receiving, not even
the carols, but the humble heart
that receives anew the
wondrous gift, the Christ.

FRANK McKIBBEN

Away from the Manger

STEPHANIE WELCHER THOMPSON

"Okay, that's the last of it," said my fiancé, Michael, as he stacked the final box in my entry hall.

I surveyed the tattered, dusty containers with anticipation. Enclosed were Christmas decorations from Michael's childhood. It was a part of his past, but to me it signified our future together as a couple. We were doing all sorts of holiday activities in unison—parties, shopping, and now decorating.

In a few months, we'd be married. I was eager to create some Christmas traditions of our own. I yearned for meaningful practices, significant and unique to our family. Opening those crates was better than Christmas.

"Look at this," Michael exclaimed over each ornament and figurine, excitedly telling me the story behind each one. His eyes shone as bright as the twinkle lights on the two-foot-tall ceramic Christmas tree. "Mom made this," he said soberly, a little wistfully.

Michael's mother died when he was nineteen, so these boxes had sat in storage the past nine years. We'd made our way through several big boxes and now came to a smaller box. A nativity scene hid inside.

"Mom always put that under the Christmas tree," Michael told me.

I carefully unwrapped the Mary and Joseph figurines and the carved wooden trough that served as a bed for the Baby Jesus. Stuffed deep in newspapers was an open barn. I placed it on the floor beneath the tree and arranged three wise men, a shepherd boy, a lamb, and a cow, all facing the manger. All the pieces were there—except the Baby Jesus.

While unpacking, I'd thrown the wrappings back in the box. I double-checked each paper, hoping to find the missing piece. But my search proved futile. Jesus was gone.

"Honey," I called to Michael who busily arranged Santa's toy shop in the dining room. "I can't find Jesus."

Michael put a hand on my shoulder. "Excuse me?" he asked playfully.

"The Baby Jesus for the nativity—He's not here," I explained, rummaging through more wrappings.

Michael's expression changed. "It's here. It has to be. We had it the last Christmas Mom was alive."

Hours later, all the boxes were unpacked. Baby Jesus never appeared. Michael sadly suggested we pack the nativity scene back in the crate.

"No, no," I said. "I'll find a baby that matches tomorrow."

We kissed goodnight and Michael went home.

The next day, I stuffed Jesus' bed into my purse and headed to the hobby store on my lunch hour. Amazed, I couldn't find a Baby Jesus there. After work, I searched for Him at several other stores. I discovered that Baby Jesus wasn't sold separately. I considered buying another nativity and using the Jesus in Michael's, but all the babies I saw were too big for the bed.

Michael came over for dinner a few days later and I broke the news to him. After we ate, I began repacking the nativity figurines in their box. Michael stopped me.

"I think we should leave it out," he said.

"Honey, we can't. There's no baby," I replied. "We can't have a nativity without Jesus."

Michael took my hand. "Stand back," he said. We walked a few feet away from the tree. "At first glance, you don't notice that the baby's not there. It's not until you look closely that you see the Christ child is missing."

I cocked my head and looked at the scene. He was right, but I didn't understand his point. Could he possibly be suggesting that as long as no one could tell the difference from a distance, it didn't matter whether there was a Baby Jesus or not?

But then he elaborated, "Amid the decorations, shopping lists, and parties, Christ can get lost at Christmas."

Thus began our first Christmas tradition, significant and unique to our family. Each year, we unpack the nativity set that has been in the Thompson family for three decades. We position the figures in their customary places, all except the Baby Jesus. The empty manger serves as a reminder for us not to let Christ get lost in the midst of celebrating Christmas.

Let us fix our eyes on Jesus, the author
and perfecter of our faith, who for the joy
set before him endured the cross, scorning its shame,
and sat down at the right hand of the throne of God.

HEBREWS 12:2

This is the month, and this the happy morn,
Wherein the Son of Heaven's eternal King,
Of wedded maid and virgin mother born,
Our great redemption from above did bring,
For so the holy sages once did sing,
That He our deadly forfeit should release,
And with His Father work us a perpetual peace.

JOHN MILTON

Dear Heavenly Father,

How can I express my gratitude for Your saving hand in my life? Thank You, Lord Jesus, for the salvation You brought to the earth. Let this season not escape me without truly celebrating and thanking You for the day of our salvation. And please show me how to reflect Your love to the people who celebrate alongside me.

Amen.

Acknowledgments

"Angel with an Accent"© Beverly Bush Smith. Used by permission. All rights reserved.

"Apple Pies and Silver Dollars"© C. Grant Endicott. Used by permission. All rights reserved.

"At Birth"© Charlotte Adelsperger. Used by permission. All rights reserved.

"Away from the Manger"© Stephanie Welcher Thompson. Used by permission. All rights reserved.

"Chocolate Kisses Before Breakfast"© Jean Stewart. Used by permission. All rights reserved.

"Christmas Crumbs"© Beverly Bush Smith. Used by permission. All rights reserved.

"The Christmas I Grew Up"© Terrence Conklin. Used by permission. All rights reserved.

"Christmas in a Refugee Camp"© Renie Burghardt. Used by permission. All rights reserved.

"A Christmas Poem"© Violet Nesdoly. Used by permission. All rights reserved.

"The Christmas Tree"© Sarah Oliver. Used by permission. All rights reserved.

"The Clock"© Esther North. Used by permission. All rights reserved.

"Cookies from Heaven"© Margaret Lang. Used by permission. All rights reserved.

"A Country Christmas"© Elaine Young McGuire. Used by permission. All rights reserved.

"Daddy's Christmas Trees"© Anne Culbreath Watkins. Used by permission. All rights reserved.

"Forever Sisters"© Nanette Thorsen-Snipes. Used by permission. All rights reserved.

"The Gift of a Lifetime"© Lydia E. Harris. Used by permission. All rights reserved.

"Gifts from the Heart"© Karen Majoris-Garrison. Used by permission. All rights reserved.

"God's Presence"© Tonya Ruiz. Used by permission. All rights reserved.

More Ways to Enjoy the Season

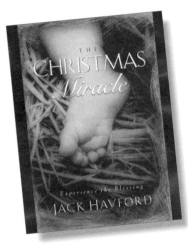

The Christmas Miracle
Experience the Blessing
Jack W. Hayford
ISBN 08307.25180

Getting Ready for Christmas
An Advent Devotional & Journal
Marty Bullis
ISBN 08307.42786